BITCHIN'
IN THE
KITCHEN:

The PMS Survival Cookbook

D1554719

BITCHIN' IN THE KITCHEN:

The PMS Survival Cookbook

~ ~ ~ ~ ~ ~

Jennifer Evans
and
Fritzi Horstman

KENSINGTON BOOKS

http://www.kensingtonbooks.com

This book is intended to be humorous. The authors and the publishers do not suggest that the recipes will actually relieve symptoms of PMS or constitute healthful eating.

KENSINGTON BOOKS are published by

Kensington Publishing Corp.
850 Third Avenue
New York, NY 10022

ISBN 1-57566-165-9

First Printing: May, 1997
10 9 8 7 6 5 4 3 2 1

Printed in the United States of America

The physiological changes in a woman's body pre-menstrually often result in hunger and specific food cravings. The most common foods craved are chocolate and salty chips. Liking chocolate per se is not a symptom of PMS, but driving out at midnight in a rainstorm to get it is indicative of having and giving into a strong craving. Doing this repeatedly shortly before you get your period is symptomatic of a premenstrual craving. If this behavior significantly interferes in your life, you have PMS.

—Michelle Harrison, M.D.
Self-Help for Premenstrual Syndrome

The main thing in cooking is not to screw up the food.

—Wolfgang Puck

To our mothers,
Dorothy Ann and Dorothy Ann

ACKNOWLEDGMENTS

We would like to acknowledge the following people: Beth Lieberman, Tracy Bernstein, Kate Meyer, and Sandra Martin, who made getting this book published possible.

We would also like to thank the following people for their loving contributions: Kira Carstensen, Todd Durham, Lee Everett, Diane Fingado, Linda Goldman, Madi Horstman, Sandra Lucchesi, Lori Maerov, Sharon Morrill, Julia Roberson, Julie Stoil, Ben Swett, Lynn Aime Weingarten, and of course, our friends and families who have always loved us in spite of our PMS.

CONTENTS

PREFACE

You may be saying, "PMS Cookbook! Who feels like cooking when they've got PMS?" Well, if you're that far gone, you can always order out. However, we have included some *very* simple recipes for those days when we're feeling so lethargic, irritable, and downright gnatty* that we can't even function, much less cook. There are recipes for all of your OTR† moods in categories such as "Salt," "Sugar," "Casseroles and Concoctions," as well as "Comfort Foods," "Cramp Foods," and "Desperado Feasts." We even have one chapter devoted entirely to CHOCOLATE. We are all too familiar with the desperate chocolate jones, as well as with bizarre, middle-of-the-night concoctions such as nachos with pickles and tutti-frutti Jell-O. Please note: Although this book has been molded to the needs of a woman on the verge, everyone in your family will love the delectable dishes that follow—that is, if they are brave enough to hang around you right now.

For those of us who have become completely incapaci-

---

*Gnatty:** That annoying and oh-so-familiar glazed mind one gets during PMS— the sensation that millions of gnats are buzzing around one's brain.
†**OTR:** (1) Of, relating to, or being "On the Rag", i.e. the state of menstruating; (2) of, relating to, or being cranky, emotional, and completely out of control.

tated at some point along the old PMS trail, we have provided
a section in each chapter entitled "Alternatives for the Incapacitated" (ALT), which describes alternative suggestions to our
recipes and, well, to cooking at all. Remember, this book was
written by women. We understand. So trust us. And because
we are women, we know that, even in your state, you may
be vaguely interested in the caloric content of the meals you
consume. Therefore, we have rated each recipe in terms of
"little piggies." Think of our happy little piggies as the Michelin
stars of the calorie world . . . in other words, one little pig
means the recipe is low in calories—in fact, it probably
shouldn't be in this book. Two pigs is still reasonable, three
is pushing it. Four pigs indicates that the dish is unabashedly
packed with fat and calories, guaranteed to add a few ounces
to your womanly physique. These ratings are provided to
give you a ballpark estimate . . . not that you do or should
care right now.

We feel certain that this will become your favorite cookbook, PMS or even Après S, or at the very least bring a smile
to your otherwise sullen visage.

This cookbook will help you get through PMS for as long
as you are lucky enough to get it. You will find it to be a
friend, a guide, and a comfort—the ultimate reference guide
to every possible PMS food excursion you could ever imagine
or desire. Enjoy.

My license plate says PMS. Nobody cuts me off.
          — Wendy Liebman

Anatomy of PMS

Brain malfunction

Swelling head

General feeling of ugliness

Facial aberrations
(aka Mount Saint Helens)

Absurd cravings

Ever-ready tears

Creases

Swollen eyelids

Hot flashes

Sensitivity to strange noises

Angry, livid expression

Mood swings

Odd behavior

Enlarged glands

Pimple on shoulder or back

Pools of oil

Huge, painful bazooka breasts—
hello, new bra size

Bloated elbows

But . . . but . . . butt

Where's my waist?

Cramps

"Poofy" tummy

Increased sexual appetite

Indigestion

No sexual appetite

Chipped nail polish

Torn, chewed cuticles

Enormous thighs—
what happened?

Swollen knee cap

Unshaved legs—
who cares?

I can't see my ankles

Feet are wide

Torn, chipped toenails

PMS Brain

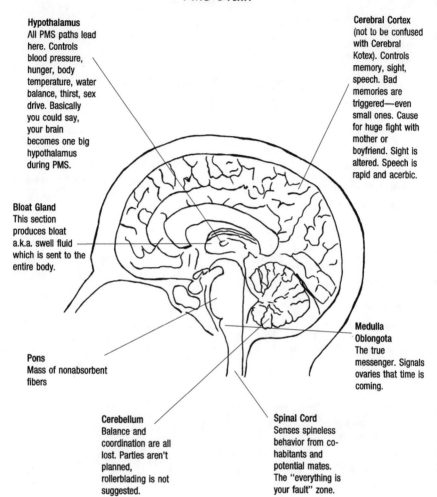

Hypothalamus
All PMS paths lead here. Controls blood pressure, hunger, body temperature, water balance, thirst, sex drive. Basically you could say, your brain becomes one big hypothalamus during PMS.

Cerebral Cortex
(not to be confused with Cerebral Kotex). Controls memory, sight, speech. Bad memories are triggered—even small ones. Cause for huge fight with mother or boyfriend. Sight is altered. Speech is rapid and acerbic.

Bloat Gland
This section produces bloat a.k.a. swell fluid which is sent to the entire body.

Medulla Oblongota
The true messenger. Signals ovaries that time is coming.

Pons
Mass of nonabsorbent fibers

Cerebellum
Balance and coordination are all lost. Parties aren't planned, rollerblading is not suggested.

Spinal Cord
Senses spineless behavior from co-habitants and potential mates. The "everything is your fault" zone.

BITCHIN' IN THE KITCHEN:

The PMS Survival Cookbook

1

CHOCOLATE

~ ~ ~ ~ ~ ~ ~

Magic Cookie Bars
Chocolate Peanut Butter Bits
Ultimate Chocolate Chip Cookies
Double Trouble Chocolate Chip Cookies
Mocha Brownies
Chocolate Cake Explosion
S'mores
Hot Fudge Sundae to Die For
Chocolate-Hazelnut Biscotti
Chocolate Satin Pie
Chocolate Mousse
Lindy Lu's Chocolate Fondue
Magic Brownies
Oatmeal Chocolate Bars
Mexican Hot Chocolate
Dottie's Quick Fudge

~ ~ ~

Swing Low, Sweet Chocolate

Chocolate. PMS. Chocolate. PMS. After a while, the two words begin to merge . . . well, with your hormones raging, they certainly appear to be a part of each other anyway. What is PMS without your favorite chocolate binge? When are you most likely to go on a chocolate spree? PMS. Chocolate. PMS . . .

In this chapter we take you from CHOCOLATE: PLAIN AND SIMPLE into the world of chocolate fantasies only a woman with PMS could dream of. From chocolate-covered-with-peanut-butter squares to chocolate brownie mix-in delight . . . you won't know whether to savor it traditionally, or immerse yourself in it physically. We give new definition to sugar shock.

You may want to accompany the following recipes with a tall glass of chocolate milk or a bottle of ripple.

Remember, chocolate is the love food: it releases the same chemicals in your body that are present when you're in love, thus duplicating that intoxicated sense of bliss. Perhaps we're all just love junkies looking for a fix. Or maybe we're just cranky. Either way, chocolate is the key.

Chocolate.

The answer to all of life's problems.

Some people like their chocolate straight. No frills, no nuts, no ice. Just chocolate. In which case we recommend the following, for that ultimate simple chocolate experience:

GHIRARDELLI	TEUSCHERS
CADBURY	DROSTE
HERSHEY'S	LINDT
GODIVA	NESTLÉ'S
TOBLER	VAN HOUTEN
VALRHONA	KRON
SEE'S	

Some of us, however, prefer our chocolate in concoction form, for which we've provided several recipes to assuage the insatiable chocolate desire.

We encourage you to roam through this book and sample the many treats that fill the pages. Just remember: You can always return to this chapter. CHOCOLATE IS ALWAYS HERE FOR YOU.

WARNING: The contents of this chapter could take you into drastic mood swings. (But since you're already on a mood swing, you might as well go as high as you can and as low as you fall. And then eat more chocolate.)

~ Magic Cookie Bars ~

Abracadabra! These bars will magically appear on your thighs faster than David Copperfield can make a rabbit appear. Even Claudia eats these when she's OTR.

½ cup butter
1½ cups graham cracker crumbs
1⅓ cups coconut
1 cup chocolate chips (more if you want)
1 cup butterscotch chips
1 cup peanut butter chips
1 cup walnuts
1 can sweetened condensed milk

Preheat oven to 350° (325° for glass pan).

In a 13 × 9 × 2 inch pan, melt butter in the oven. Sprinkle graham cracker crumbs over butter, mix until well blended. Add coconut, chips, and nuts. Cover entire pan with condensed milk. Bake 25–30 minutes, until lightly browned.

ALT: If you really can't manage to put these ingredients together, try this: Open your mouth wide, throw a couple of chocolate chips in, some graham cracker crumbs, walnuts, and a pinch of coconut, and chew them all together.

MALE TIP: Accept everything she says as law.

~ Chocolate Peanut Butter Bits ~

Here's an easy one. We recommend you eat the whole batch. It will probably make you feel sick. But anything to distract you from the gnattiness, right?

¾ cup brown sugar
1 pound confectioners sugar
1 stick butter
1 cup unsalted peanuts
12 ounces semisweet chocolate chips
1 tablespoon butter

Mix first four ingredients together. Pat into an ungreased jelly roll pan, about 15 × 10 inches and 1 inch deep.

Melt chocolate chips and butter in a double boiler. Spread chocolate on peanut butter mixture. Chill for 15–20 minutes. Cut into bite-sized squares. Remove from pan. Serve chilled.

ALT: A Hershey bar and a jar of peanut butter. Play the "Hey, you got peanut butter on my chocolate" game. Or buy some Reese's Peanut Butter Cups (the large bag) and forget this whole thing.

MALE TIP: Do not encourage her to wear that sexy G-string you bought her on Valentine's Day.

~ Ultimate Chocolate Chip Cookies ~

Better than Mrs. Fields. Seriously.

1 cup butter (2 sticks), room temperature
1 cup sugar
1 cup brown sugar
2 eggs
1½ teaspoons vanilla
2 cups flour
2½ cups oatmeal, ground in a food processor to a
   flour consistency
½ teaspoon salt
1 teaspoon baking soda
1 teaspoon baking powder
7 ounces chocolate bar, ground to flakes
12 ounces chocolate chips
1½ cups chopped nuts, lightly toasted

Combine butter and sugars until well blended. Add eggs and vanilla. In a separate bowl, combine flour, oatmeal, salt, baking soda, and baking powder. Add to butter mixture. Add chocolate flakes, chips, and nuts. Scoop out into golfball-sized balls and eat.

ALT: You can also *bake* the cookies. Put dough balls on cookie sheet, giving cookies room to expand. Bake at 375° for 8–10 minutes, until golden.

My doctor said I've got good news and I've got bad news. The good news is you don't have premenstrual syndrome. The bad news is you're a bitch.

—*Rhonda Bates*

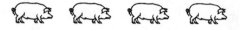

～ Double Trouble Chocolate Chip Cookies ～

When no amount of chocolate is too much . . . Try them dipped in chocolate (See "Lindy Lu's Chocolate Fondue") for the ultimate chocolate rush.

1¾ cups flour
¼ teaspoon baking soda
1 cup butter, room temperature
1 cup sugar
½ cup dark brown sugar
1 teaspoon vanilla
1 large egg
⅓ cup unsweetened powdered cocoa
2 tablespoons milk
6 ounces chocolate chips
1 cup walnuts

Preheat oven to 350°.

Combine flour and baking soda. In separate bowl, cream butter, sugars, and vanilla. Add egg. Combine cocoa and milk and add to butter mixture. Combine the flour into the butter/cocoa mixture. Add chocolate chips and walnuts. Bake 12 minutes.

ALT: Nestlé Toll House refrigerated cookie dough—just slice 'em off and bake them, one at a time, or well, who's kidding who? Just cram the entire log of dough into your mouth.

MALE TIP: Do not mention the word "irrational."

~ Mocha Brownies ~

Has anyone ever mentioned the effects of caffeine and chocolate on a female with PMS? Putting that aside, here is a recipe which expertly combines two of our favorite flavors— coffee and chocolate.

5 ounces unsweetened chocolate
1 rounded tablespoon powdered instant espresso
1 cup butter
1¾ cups brown sugar
5 eggs
2 tablespoons vanilla
1 cup flour
1 cup toasted almonds, chopped
⅔ cup chopped chocolate chips

Preheat oven to 350°.

Grease a 13 × 9 × 2-inch pan. Melt chocolate on low heat, stir in espresso powder. Cool.

In a large bowl cream sugar and butter. Add eggs, one at a time, beating well after each. Blend in vanilla. Add chocolate mixture.

Stir in flour gradually. Fold in almonds and chocolate chips. Nibble at the chips by the handful, but save some for the brownies.

Bake 20–30 minutes, until knife comes out clean. Cool before consuming.

ALT: Duncan Hines, Pillsbury, etc. Mix, bake, and eat right out of the pan with a cup of Java on the side.

It is possible that blondes also prefer gentlemen.
                                        —*Mamie Van Doren*

~ Chocolate Cake Explosion ~

THE EASY AND AWESOME WAY. This is a particularly good cake to eat raw, with your fingers, in front of the TV. Who's gonna know? (Makes a nice dip, too.)

Cake

> **1 box cake mix**
> **1 box of chocolate pudding**
> **1 12-ounce package of chocolate chips**
> **1 can of frosting or the recipe below**

Follow directions on cake mix box to make batter. Add pudding mix. Blend together. Spread half of batter into a 13 × 9 × 2-inch pan. Add chips. Cover with remaining batter. Bake according to directions on cake mix box. Frost. Eat.

Chocolate Frosting

> **8 tablespoons (1 stick) butter, room temperature**
> **1½ cups semisweet chocolate chips**
> **1 teaspoon vanilla**
> **1⅓ cups confectioners sugar**

Melt butter and chocolate in a heavy sauce pan over low heat. Remove pan from heat, add vanilla. Transfer mixture to a mixing bowl or just mix in the pan, adding sugar gradually with an electric mixer.

Chill for 1 hour, beating every 15 minutes. The icing will get stiff. Spread on cake. Eat. Wash down with a quart of milk.

ALT: If you're really out of sorts and can't bake your own cake, have a HOHO. It should do the trick.

Telltale PMS Symptom: You cry at Puppy Chow commercials.

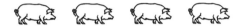

~ S'mores ~

You remember these from camp, right? Well, like its sister, the Rice Krispie Treat, the s'more takes on a whole new meaning when you've got PMS . . .

1 box graham crackers
Hershey bars (a dozen or so will do nicely)
bag of marshmallows
Peanut butter (optional nineties version)

Lay out two crackers and a slice of chocolate (and peanut butter, if you like).

Heat marshmallow over open flame using stick or fork.*

When marshmallow is toasty (or burned, if you're that type), stick in between the two graham crackers and wedge of chocolate. Press together, let chocolate melt. Eat.

ALT: There is a cereal called S'mores. Eat it out of the box. Since you can't be bothered to leave the couch, bring it to your resting area and consume as desired.

MALE TIP: Do not mention how filthy the house is.

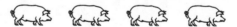

---

*Do not burn your tongue on the fork!! Frying your taste buds will *not* help your mood.

~ Hot Fudge Sundae to Die For ~

1 pint of your favorite flavor of Häagen-Dazs
hot fudge sauce (homemade or from the gourmet
** store)**
toasted chopped nuts (walnuts, almonds, pecans . . .)
whipped cream
cherry (optional)

Dump the pint of Häagen-Dazs into a large mixing bowl. Heat fudge sauce through. Pour over ice cream. Add plenty of nuts. Top with whipped cream and, if you're in the mood, a cherry. Indulge. Go wild. Smear it all over your body. It's chocolate.

ALT: There is no alternative.

A waist is a terrible thing to mind.

—*Jane Caminos*

~ Chocolate-Hazelnut Biscotti ~

The added crunch in these will help you get out your aggression. The chocolate will soothe your nerves. The nuts will keep you nuts.

1 stick butter
¾ cup sugar
2 eggs
1 teaspoon vanilla
2¼ cups unbleached flour
1½ teaspoons baking powder
¼ teaspoon salt
¾ cup semisweet chocolate, finely chopped
½ cup hazelnuts, skinned, toasted, and chopped

Preheat oven to 325°.

Cream butter with sugar. Add eggs and vanilla. In a separate bowl, combine flour, baking powder, and salt. Add to butter mixture and combine. (Do not overmix.) Add chocolate and nuts.

Separate the dough into three equal sections. On a lightly floured surface, roll sections into long logs, about 2 inches in diameter. Bake on baking sheet for 25 minutes, until golden brown.

Cool the logs and slice diagonally to make ½- to ¾-inch-thick biscotti slices. Lower oven to 250°. Put the slices on baking sheet and bake for 20 minutes. Turn the slices over and bake for another 20 minutes.

ALT: Any stale cookies you have lying around. Just make sure they're rock hard. (Also good to throw at a nearby "aggravator.")

Edgar Berman, M.D., came to national attention in the late 1960s when he declared that a woman president could be dangerously unstable because she was subject to a "raging hormonal imbalance."

~ Chocolate Satin Pie ~

Thick, rich, and delicious—and oh, so easy. A must for die-hard chocoholics with PMS, seeking a chocolate jolt. Dive into this pie head first. Come up for air only when you're done.

1½ cups evaporated milk
2 egg yolks
2 cups semisweet chocolate chips
1 prepared chocolate crumb crust
whipped cream
chopped walnuts

In a 2-quart saucepan, over medium heat, whisk evaporated milk and egg yolks, stirring constantly. Thicken slightly. Remove from heat and stir in chocolate chips until chips are completely melted and very smooth. Pour into crust. Chill until firm. Top with whipped cream and sprinkle with nuts.

ALT: Oreos, chocolate pudding, and Cool Whip. In your mouth. In any order. Anytime, anyplace.

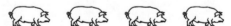

~ Chocolate Mousse ~

One of our favorite ways to ingest, enjoy, and pay homage to the Goddess of Chocolate.

24 ounces of semisweet chocolate chips
½ cup prepared espresso coffee
½ cup Kahlúa
4 egg yolks
1 cup heavy cream, chilled
¼ cup sugar
8 egg whites
Pinch of salt

In a heavy saucepan, melt chocolate chips, stirring constantly. Add espresso and Kahlúa. Stir until incorporated. Cool to room temperature. Add egg yolks, one at a time, until well blended.

Whip heavy cream until thick. Gradually beat in sugar, beating until stiff. In a separate bowl, beat egg whites with salt until stiff. Gently fold egg whites into cream.

Stir one third of whipped cream and egg white mixture thoroughly into chocolate mixture. Then scrape remaining cream and egg mixture over lightened chocolate mixture and fold together. Be gentle. The egg whites want to keep their fluffiness. Pour into a serving bowl. Chill for about 2 hours.

ALT: Swiss Miss Chocolate Pudding Snacks.

MALE TIP: Don't invite your pals over for "Monday Night Football."

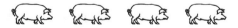

~ Lindy Lu's Chocolate Fondue ~

Our dear friend Linda Loves chocolate on everything. And so do we. Here's our "fondue" recipe and some creative dipping suggestions.

12 ounces semisweet chocolate
1 tablespoon oil

In a 2-quart sauce pan melt the chocolate with the oil, stirring constantly until smooth. Pour chocolate sauce into fondue pot surrounded by your various dipping items.

Dipping Items

Chocolate bar
Strawberries
Bananas
Almonds
Bread
Carrot sticks
Peanut butter
Oreos
Biscotti
Pretzels
Pickles
Corn flakes
Cap'n Crunch
Marshmallows
Apples
Walnuts
Hazelnuts
Pecans
Mini-corncobs
Graham crackers
Chocolate chip cookies
Chocolate chips
Olives
Potato chips
Popcorn
Your boyfriend!

In case you haven't noticed: ANYTHING IS GOOD WHEN IT'S DIPPED IN CHOCOLATE!

When he is late for dinner and I know he must be either having an affair or lying dead in the street, I always hope he's dead.

—*Judith Viorst*

~ Magic Brownies ~

What can be easier than brownies? And these brownies can be whatever you want them to be. Gooey turtle brownies, or choc-full of chocolate Oreo cookie brownies. Be creative and make up your own. If you don't want to be creative, we don't care. Follow our ideas or just skip this whole thing. We don't want to annoy you.

4 ounces unsweetened chocolate
1½ sticks butter
2 cups sugar
3 eggs
1½ teaspoons vanilla
1 cup flour
1 cup nuts (optional)

Melt chocolate with butter, stirring constantly. Add sugar to chocolate mixture, blend lightly. Add eggs and vanilla and mix well. Add flour and nuts. Stir until blended. Spread into 13 × 9 × 2-inch greased pan. Bake at 350° for 35–40 minutes.

Variations

Oreo brownies:	Crumble 10–15 Oreos on top of brownies before baking.
M&M brownies:	Sprinkle your favorite M&M's on top.
Heath Bar brownies:	Buy the pieces or make your own pieces.

Turtle brownies: Melt 1½ cups of caramel pieces
                          in a sauce pan and spread on
                          brownies before baking. Throw
                          the caramel pan away. Sprinkle
                          with 1 cup pecans.

ALT: Put Oreos, M&M's, Heathbars, pecans, and caramels
in a bowl. Eat with spoon or hands. Oh yeah. If you want
the brownies, either make 'em or buy the Sara Lee frosted
kind and throw them in the bowl as well.

*MALE TIP: Godiva chocolates may bring out the best in
her right now. Bring some home.*

~ Oatmeal Chocolate Bars ~

It's a cookie and a bar. A bar and a cookie. A cookie bar. Getting annoyed? Want to hit us? Well, you can't. We're thousands of miles away. We're authors of a cookbook and you don't know where we live. So take it out on your loved ones. Hee-hee. The chewy crunchiness of these bars will soothe any irritation the creation of these has precipitated.

Cookie Base

½ cup butter
1 cup brown sugar
1 egg
1 teaspoon vanilla
1¼ cups flour
½ teaspoon baking soda
2 cups rolled oats (e.g., Quaker)

Mix butter, sugar, and egg until creamy. Add vanilla, flour, and soda until blended. Stir in oats.

Filling

2 tablespoons butter
6 ounces semisweet chocolate chips
1 can evaporated milk (5⅓ ounces)
¼ cup sugar
½ cup chopped nuts

In a heavy sauce pan, combine butter, chips, evaporated milk and sugar to a rolling boil, stirring constantly. Remove from heat, add nuts and cool.

Press ⅔ of cookie base to a 9-inch square pan. Spread with ¾ of the filling. In a separate bowl combine remaining filling with remaining cookie base. Crumble on top of filling. Bake at 350° for 25–30 minutes. Cool, then cut into bars.

ALT: Oatmeal cookies (without raisins) dipped in melted chocolate (6 ounces chocolate chips melted in a sauce pan with 1 tablespoon oil). You can get a pot holder and dip in the pan while watching your favorite "Bewitched" rerun. Try twitching your nose and all the cookies will disappear.

MALE TIP: Hide the knives and other sharp instruments. Just in case.

~ Mexican Hot Chocolate ~

What better way to consume a lot of chocolate and a lot of dairy? We've added cream to this concoction to give you some added calories. Serve with a flan or with cookies or toast. *Olé.*

2 ounces unsweetened chocolate
2 cups milk
1 cup heavy cream
7 tablespoons sugar
½ teaspoon cinnamon
1 egg
1 teaspoon vanilla

In a double boiler, melt chocolate. In a separate saucepan, heat milk and cream until hot, but not boiling. Take ¼ cup of hot milk and add to chocolate until they form a smooth paste. Add the rest of the milk, sugar, and cinnamon.

Beat egg and vanilla. Add 2 tablespoons of chocolate mixture to egg slowly, mixing well. Add egg to chocolate mixture. With the double boiler still on low heat, beat chocolate mixture with a rotary beater for about 3 minutes.

ALT: Milk and Bosco or Hershey's Syrup. Little marshmallows on top might make you happier.

Good communication is as stimulating as black coffee, and just as hard to sleep after.

—*Anne Morrow Lindbergh*

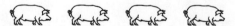

~ Dottie's Quick Fudge ~

Sometimes you want it fast, but fudge usually takes a while. Not Dottie's Quick Fudge. You should be able to make this fudge within fifteen minutes, if you do it right. And now for the magic words: *No thermometer needed.*

2 cups sugar
3 tablespoons Hershey's Cocoa (or more for richer flavor)
1 cup milk
glob of butter (about 2 tablespoons)
chopped nuts (optional)
1 teaspoon vanilla

Put sugar, cocoa, and milk into a saucepan and boil until mixture forms a soft ball in a glass of water. Toss in glob of butter, chopped nuts, and vanilla. Cool pan in sink half-full of cold water. Pour into buttered dish quickly, before it solidifies. Let cool and cut into squares. You can also eat it straight from the pan. Fast and furious calories for the chocoholic on the run.

It's the good girls who keep the diaries; the bad girls never have the time.

—*Tallulah Bankhead*

2

COMFORT FOODS

~ ~ ~ ~ ~ ~

Meatloaf Like Mom Used to Make
Extra-Garlicky Mashed Potatoes with Southern Gravy
Jen's Favorite Chicken Pot Pie
Chicken Fried Steak with Gravy
Homemade Chicken and Dumplings à la Fritzi's
Mom and Elvis
Creamy Creamed Spinach
The Best Peanut Butter and Jelly Sandwich
in the World
Jell-O
Luscious Pasta Alfredo
Mongo Burrito
Polenta with Mushrooms
Pecan-Buttermilk Waffles
Chopped Liver
Blueberry Cornmeal Pancakes
Rice Pudding
Tapioca Pudding
Sharon's Once-a-Month Vodka Martini

~ ~ ~

It's a gray day outside . . . and inside. You've got the blues. Your uterus aches. A pimple has suddenly appeared on your normally pristine complexion. You feel lonely, cranky, sad, unloved, misunderstood. You want your mommy. But your mommy lives fifteen hundred miles away in Tahlequah, Oklahoma, or someplace like that, and all you've got is yourself. And your kitchen. That's why God invented "comfort foods." You know what they are. It's usually the stuff we were force-fed as children. Now we crave it. Take that to your shrink. Each person has his or her own idea of the perfect comfort food. My comfort food of choice is mashed potatoes. Perhaps yours is Ritz Crackers with Cheez Whiz. We have taken the liberty of giving you a sample of some of our favorite comfort dishes. So, put on that puffy robe and those fluffy slippers you wouldn't normally be caught dead in, and snuggle up with one of the following . . .

~ Meat Loaf Like Mom Used to Make ~

Okay, Mom, your secret is out. Now we know why you served meatloaf *once a month*. Just like clockwork. Think of this recipe as sort of a passing of the torch . . . er, loaf. Enjoy, O fellow carnivore lasses.

1 pound ground beef
1 egg yolk
Worcestershire sauce*
1 tablespoon bread crumbs
1 tablespoon chopped garlic
⅛ cup chopped onion
¼ cup ketchup
salt and pepper to taste

Mush ground beef, egg, Worcestershire sauce, bread crumbs, garlic, and onion together with your bare hands (very therapeutic). Form it into a loaf shape and stuff it into a loaf pan. Pour ketchup on top, add dash of salt and pepper, and bake at 350° for about 40 minutes, or until it looks done. Eat with a huge mound of garlic mashed potatoes (recipe follows). Don't even think about counting calories right now. You may also use your hands.

If you have it, a full-bodied red wine goes well with this dish. If not, Thunderbird will do just fine.

---

*Do *not* try to spell this in your present condition.

ALT: Go to McDonalds, get a burger, take the bun off, and add ketchup.

There is no love sincerer than the love of food.
                                      —*George Bernard Shaw*

~ Extra-Garlicky Mashed Potatoes with Southern Gravy ~

Rich, creamy, and warm. The ultimate comfort food.

Potatoes

- **2 pounds potatoes**
- **4 cloves garlic**
- **¼ cup milk or cream**
- **4 tablespoons butter (only real butter will do—no Weight Watchers, please)**
- **salt and pepper to taste**

Boil potatoes and garlic until tender, about 30 minutes. Drain. Place in large bowl and mash with milk/cream, butter, salt, and pepper to desired consistency. For creamier potatoes, add more milk. (If you have the energy, you can bake the garlic or caramelize it on the side first, then add it as you are mashing potatoes.)

Gravy

- **2 tablespoons olive oil or grease drippings**
- **2 tablespoons flour**
- **1 clove of garlic, finely chopped (optional)**
- **1 cup plus 2 tablespoons milk**
- **salt and pepper to taste**

Make a roux: Combine olive oil or grease drippings with flour. If you want, you can finely chop a clove of garlic and sauté it at this point. Stir over medium heat until smooth. Add milk, salt, and pepper. Add more milk or flour, as necessary. You've got the basic idea. Pour steaming gravy over mounds of delicious potatoes. You're home.

ALT: Put on dark glasses, go to KFC, order double mashed potatoes and gravy. Pretend not to recognize any of the other women in dark glasses pigging out on same.

It is only trifles that irritate my nerves.
—*Queen Victoria of England*

~ Jen's Favorite Chicken Pot Pie ~

High in fat, dairy, and salt, this dish is a natural for the PMS victim. Ahhh, there's nothing like this golden crust-covered, creamy dream of comforting chicken and veggies when you're feeling out of sorts. Yeah, well, dream on. You're in no shape to create the gourmet version of this pie, so to save you some angst, we went straight to the alternative on this one.

ALT: Swanson's still has those little chicken pot pies in the frozen food section. The little foil containers are great for crunching up in one's fist in pain and/or anger later.

MALE TIP: Do not suggest a day at the beach in her new bikini.

~ Chicken Fried Steak with Gravy ~

Head 'em up and mooooo-ve 'em out, cowgirls! You may need a fix of this old Southern favorite to cure the PMS blues. Hands down, one of the greasiest entrées this side of the Rio Grande. *Mmmmm.*

Tenderized cube steak (however much you want)
1 egg, beaten with a little milk
flour
salt and pepper
cooking oil

Steak

Tenderize meat a bit more by piercing it with fork, etc., getting those nasty aggressions out. Coat with egg/milk mixture, then quickly dredge with flour. Season with salt and pepper. Fry until just cooked in hot cooking oil in frying pan. Then bake at 350° until crispy and golden brown, about ten minutes.

Gravy

meat drippings
2 tablespoons flour
2 cups milk or cream for gravy
salt and pepper to taste

After removing steaks from pan, add about 2 tablespoons of flour and stir with grease and browned crispy particles.

Continue cooking and stirring roux (i.e., flour/grease mixture) until smooth, then add milk or cream to make gravy. Add salt and pepper. Pour over steak and enjoy. Southern comfort food at it's best.

ALT: Smother a hamburger patty with a can of Franco-American chicken gravy. Pretend it's the real thing.

Never eat more than you can lift.

—*Miss Piggy*

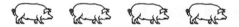

~ Homemade Chicken and Dumplings à la Fritzi's Mom and Elvis ~

Like all the butter in this recipe, this dish will melt in your mouth, on your napkin, into your thighs. It is the ultimate in comfort decadence. The King knew how to eat. Generations of PMS women can now follow his footsteps. Long live the King.

Chicken

> **1 stick of butter**
> **1 preroasted chicken**
> **garlic salt**
> **pepper**
> **ground sage**
> **1 can cream of chicken soup**
> **½ can water**
> **1 teaspoon Tabasco sauce**
> **1 teaspoon Worcestershire sauce**

In a large skillet, melt butter. Add pieces of roasted chicken, garlic salt, pepper, and sage. Sauté for a few minutes. In a separate bowl, dump in can of cream of chicken soup, water, Worcestershire, and Tabasco. Pour over browned chicken. Cover and simmer on low heat for 35 minutes.

Dumplings

2 cups sifted self-rising cake flour*
¾ cup milk
2 tablespoons melted butter
½ teaspoon onion salt
**½ teaspoon caraway seeds (optional—we prefer
without)**

Combine all ingredients, mixing lightly. After chicken has simmered for 10 minutes, drop dumpling mixture by the teaspoon into simmering liquid.

DUMPLING NOTE: If you want more dumplings (PIG), here's Mom's suggestion: Create an identical cream of chicken soup, water, Worcestershire, and Tabasco mixture, boil in separate sauce pan, and double dumpling recipe. That way you are sure to have enough dumplings.

ALT: Boil some canned chicken soup, tear off pieces of Popin Fresh Dough, and toss into soup. Cook until dumplings float to the top.

MALE TIP: Wear a jock strap or a protective athletic cup.

---

*We suggest that you don't spend too much time tracking this down. If you don't see it on the shelf, regular enriched flour will work.

~ Creamy Creamed Spinach ~

You may wish to slather this glorious, creamy concoction onto your body for a quick, at-home spa treatment. We like to eat it. Anytime, anyplace.

2 pounds fresh spinach
3 tablespoons butter
5 tablespoons flour
2 cups milk
½ teaspoon salt
fresh ground pepper
dash nutmeg

Wash spinach well and chop finely. Cook in a large saucepan until just wilted. Heat butter in a skillet. Add flour, stir until brown. Add milk until thick and smooth. Add spinach. Add salt, pepper, and nutmeg to taste.

ALT: Dump 1 can of spinach, some milk, and a pinch of garlic salt into a bowl. Microwave on high. Stir and eat. Feeling better?

Could you please just leave me alone?

—*J. Evans*

~ The Best Peanut Butter and Jelly Sandwich in the World ~

Warning: The following may stick to the roof of your mouth and cause difficulty in whining, resulting in a severe temper tantrum. Prepare only in early stages of PMS.

homemade bread
peanut butter
raspberry preserves
fresh raspberries
crushed peanuts

Spread peanut butter and raspberry preserves on thick slices of bread, slightly toasted. Sprinkle some fresh raspberries and crushed peanuts on top. Eat immediately with large glass of cold milk.

ALT: Wonder Bread and Smucker's Peanut Butter and Grape Jelly Swirl. Dip the bread into the jar of Smucker's. Wash down with vodka.

MALE TIP: Check your calendar. She may not know it (or have conveniently forgotten in the heat of the moment) but that erratic behavior and ridiculously hostile fight may be signs of PMS.

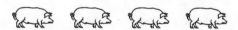

~ Jell-O ~

There's always room for Jell-O. Even with that bloated, premenstrual tummy of yours. The good news is, this stuff is fat-free. Go to town.

Add 2 cups boiling water to the gelatin of your choice. Stir until dissolved, about 2 minutes. Add 2 cups cold water. Chill until set.

Some of you may want to add fruit, cream, chocolate, or marshmallow bits. Anything, as long as it makes you happy. Go wild. Make it really disgusting and use it as a weapon.

ALT: Go to a nearby hospital. Check in. Eat your Jell-O—get mellow.

NOTE: Jell-O is also good to squish in your mouth. It will distract you for a while.

MALE TIP: Don't ask for sex. Give her sex if she wants it. Things could get crazy.

~ Luscious Pasta Alfredo ~

This may be a little ambitious for you, but we thought we'd give this to you just because it has so much DAIRY in it. Ah yes, dairy heaven, which is just what you need when you've got PMS, right? That and a lot of caffeine should just about throw you over the edge at this point. So what? Go for it.

1 cup mushrooms (optional)
1 tablespoon olive oil
garlic (2–6 cloves, depending on how bad you want
    your breath to be)
½ stick butter (ah, throw the whole stick in)
2 cups sour cream
¼ cup Parmesan cheese
juice of 1 lemon
2–3 tablespoons vermouth (or white wine)
basil (fresh or dried) and/or Italian seasonings
salt and pepper to taste
pinch nutmeg
dry pasta of your choice

Sauté mushrooms in olive oil. Add garlic and sauté (do not overcook). Add butter, sour cream, shredded Parmesan cheese, lemon, and vermouth. Cook on low heat until blended and creamy. Add chopped basil and a large pinch of the herbs. Add salt and cracked pepper to taste, and the pinch of nutmeg.

Cook pasta until done. Toss with creamy sauce. Eat with a delicious Chardonnay or Beaujolais. This is one you can invite friends over to share—they'll thank you, that is, unless they're on diets.

ALT: Contadina or other fresh pasta and Alfredo Sauce. You can find them at your favorite grocery store.

The trouble with eating Italian food is that 5 or 6 days later you'll be hungry again.

—*George Miller*

~ Mongo Burrito ~

This burrito is so comforting, you may even want to wrap yourself inside the soft, warm folds of the tortilla. Come to think of it, maybe you should invite a friend.

small handful onions
⅛ cup peppers (red, green)
2 tablespoons olive oil
½ cup black beans (cooked)
large flour tortilla (or a dozen, depending on how ravenous and/or self-destructive you're feeling)
½ cup rice (cook per instructions)
½ cup shredded chicken (precooked)
big handful of cheddar and jack cheese
3 tablespoons salsa
¼ cup sour cream
½ cup guacamole (*see* recipe, p. 98)

Sauté onions and peppers in olive oil. Set aside. Heat black beans through. Spread tortilla flat on surface of baking dish. Fill with black beans, rice, sautéed onions and peppers, chicken. Sprinkle cheese and salsa on top of mixture. Wrap tortilla around mixture, tucking edges inside. Bake at 400° for about 10–15 minutes, until cheese is nice and melted. Top with sour cream and guacamole. Pig out.

ALT: Two words: Taco Bell.

Euphemisms:
   That time of the month
   Getting my period

Having the monthlies
On the rag
The curse
Aunt Red
Friend from Red Bank
Fallen off the roof
Aunt Flo
Riding the cotton pony
My friend is visiting

~ Polenta with Mushrooms ~

Like mushy cornbread, this wonderful Italian peasant dish is a natural comfort food. Dump the creamy mushroom mixture over it and enjoy.

2 cups mushrooms
2 tablespoons butter
3 cloves garlic, mashed
½ cup cream or sour cream
¼ cup parmesan cheese
salt and pepper to taste
couple of drops of lemon
1 box polenta
chicken broth/bouillon

Preheat oven to 325°.

Sauté mushrooms in butter and garlic until soft. Add cream, about 3 tablespoons of parmesan cheese, salt, and pepper. Stir and simmer. Do not use high heat—cream will curdle. Squeeze a couple drops of lemon in.

Meanwhile, prepare polenta according to instructions on box. Instead of boiling it in water, use chicken stock or bouillon. Pour into a 13 × 9 × 2-inch pan, sprinkle with Parmesan cheese to cover, and bake until slightly golden brown, 15–20 minutes. Let it cool and top with warm mushroom mixture. *Mmmmmmm.*

ALT: Instant polenta requires 5 minutes—all you have to do is stir. You can handle that, can't you?

MALE TIP: Do not stay out late with the boys.

~ Pecan-Buttermilk Waffles ~

The pecans in these waffles are good for crunching out that PMS *morning* angst. Dump a slab of warm butter and some maple syrup on your waffle—you may be a morning person after all.

pancake mix (e.g., Bisquick)
egg
milk
pecan halves
maple syrup*

Preheat waffle iron and grease lightly. In a large mixing bowl combine all ingredients. Use ⅓ cup per waffle. Set to desired heat and pour it on. Serve with warm maple syrup and decorate with extra pecan halves.

ALT: We like Eggo frozen waffles with Mrs. Butterworth's syrup.

MALE TIP: This is not the time to bring up any outstanding issues.

---

*Low in fat (like you really care).

~ Chopped Liver ~

"You never write, you never call. What am I, chopped liver?" At this point, you should be so lucky to be chopped liver, because it's the perfect PMS comfort food. You need your iron, honey, so stop whining and eat your liver. And call your mother.

1 pound chicken livers
¼ cup olive oil
2 cups chopped onions
4 hard-cooked eggs, peeled and chopped
⅓ cup mayonnaise
salt
freshly ground pepper

Wash livers, discard fat, etc. Heat oil in skillet, add chopped onions, stir until translucent, stir in livers, and cook about 7–8 minutes. Set aside.

Put liver mixture and eggs into food processor fitted with steel blade. Process until mixture is smooth. Scrape into bowl and add mayonnaise, salt, and pepper. Serve with crusty bread or crackers. We also like to add chopped liver to turkey sandwiches, or on top of raisin toast. Other than the extremely high fat content, this dish is actually good for you.

ALT: Any kind of prewrapped pâté—we prefer pâté de foie gras with truffles.

Show me a woman who doesn't feel guilty and I'll show you a man.

—*Erica Jong*

~ Blueberry Cornmeal Pancakes ~

Good morning, gorgeous. Feeling hungry? Thought so. These are quick and easy to make. The blueberries sometimes make the batter look purple, so be prepared. If you don't like purple pancakes, forget the blueberries. If you don't like cornmeal, forget the pancakes. But if this sounds good to you (it's one of our favorites), then make the whole batch and smother with loads of butter and maple syrup.

1 cup cornmeal
1 cup unbleached white flour
2 teaspoons baking powder
½ teaspoon baking soda
½ teaspoon salt
2 eggs
2 cups milk
2 tablespoons canola oil
1 cup blueberries (fresh is better, frozen will do)
butter or oil for frying

Combine dry ingredients in one bowl. In another bowl, beat eggs, then add milk and oil. Mix wet ingredients with dry ingredients. Gently add blueberries. Cook on skillet using either butter or oil.

ALT: Aunt Jemima's Pancake & Waffle Mix. Add blueberries before frying. And if you don't like purple pancakes, see above.

Telltale PMS Symptom: You no longer have the patience of a saint.

~ Rice Pudding ~

Hey, Puddin'. There's something about rice pudding that makes everything okay. Even in your crazy condition, this rice pudding will put a smile on your face. Sink into the creaminess, the raisins, the high fat content. Yum.

2 tablespoons butter
3½ cups milk
¼ cup sugar
½ cup brown or white rice (cooked)
1½ vanilla beans
1 cinnamon stick
1 egg yolk
2 tablespoons water
⅔ cup raisins
cinnamon

In a very big pot or saucepan, put butter, milk, sugar, rice, vanilla beans, and cinnamon stick. Bring to a boil, reduce heat, and simmer 8 minutes, stirring every 2–3 minutes.

Combine egg yolk and water, then stir into milk/rice mixture. Simmer for 12 minutes longer. Remove from heat and transfer to separate container and chill in fridge. Stir every 10 minutes to prevent the feisty rice grains from settling on the bottom.

Simmer raisins in the water for 2 minutes or until puffy. Let cool for 1 hour then add to pudding. Refrigerate 2–3 hours. Sprinkle with cinnamon.

ALT: Make some toast. Boil some milk. Combine. Sprinkle with sugar, to taste. This combo won't have the creamy-ricey feeling you were hoping for, but it has the same amount of soothing points. You could throw in some leftover rice or Cheerios for added texture.

HINT: Using heavy cream instead of milk increases the calorie content and the soothing feeling. Remember: 1 gram of fat = 1 soothing point. Go for 100 grams. You'll be so soothed, you'll be in a coma.

MALE TIP: This is not the time to remind her of her New Year's resolutions.

~ Tapioca Pudding ~

Do you know what tapioca is? Bet you don't. Bet you don't. Nah, nah, nah.

Most people don't know that tapioca is a granular preparation of the cassava plant. Most people don't care either.

Make some. It'll put you in touch with the cassava plant.

3 tablespoons quick-cooking tapioca
¼ cup sugar
2 tablespoons honey
¼ teaspoon salt
2 eggs
2 cups milk

Combine all ingredients in a medium sauce pan and whisk to blend. Let stand, without stirring or cooking, for about 5 minutes. Cook over medium heat, stirring until mixture comes to a full boil.

Transfer to a medium bowl set over a bowl of ice water. Let stand to cool, stirring occasionally, 10–15 minutes. Makes four servings—all for you.

ALT: Hunt's Snack Pack.

Telltale PMS Symptom: Everything seems upside down, backwards, and surreal.

～ Sharon's Once-a-Month Vodka Martini ～

ice
vodka (Sharon prefers Ketel One)
dry vermouth
2 olives

Put ice in your favorite martini glass to chill glass. Fill martini shaker with ice cubes. Pour 2 ounces or more (depending on mood) of your favorite vodka into shaker. Add a very small dash of dry vermouth.

Shake the mixture. How hard and how long also depends on your mood. Let it all out, ladies.

After emptying ice out of martini glass, strain drink into your chilled glass. Add two olives. Sip or gulp your drink—whatever feels appropriate.

Repeat above steps as necessary.

Telltale PMS Symptom: You have a sudden desire to wear white.

3
SUGAR, SUGAR

Snicker Doodles
Pecan Pie
Raspberry Tart
Pear and Apple Tarte Tatin
Fritzi's Ex's Mother's Concord Grape Pie
Cheesecake
Mexican Wedding Cake Cookies
Peanut Butter Cookies
Lemon Squares
Strawberry Shortcake
Rice Krispies Treats

Sugar and spice and everything nice. Sugar is definitely nice. Make that better than nice, for those of us with a sweet tooth.

Boys are rotten, stuffed with cotton, girls are dandy, made of candy. Perhaps that's why sweets are tops on our list when our feminine hormones begin to rumble.

What would we do without sugar? How would we soothe our sweet tooth? Luckily we don't have to worry about that. All we have to do is discover the various forms we can put sugar in.

Believe it or not, there are actually people who prefer salt (Jennifer) to sugar (Fritzi) during PMS. Naturally, this is a freaky phenomenon and not really understood by the sweet-toothed women. We're all entitled to our opinions, after all. Just give me my sugar, and I'll leave you all to your salt (more for me).

In this chapter we pay respect and homage to the God of Sugar Cane. Now bow your heads and pray:

Oh God of Sugar Cane
Bring forth your sweetness
Deliver us from the craziness of PMS
and soothe our sweet tooth.

We promise to buy sugar in its various forms
and to eat it and cook it
when the urge occurs.

We thank you for your sweetness
as you are in almost everything.

Roll your sleeves up and get your aprons on, 'cause "Suga,"
you're in for the sugar fix of your life!

Hello, I'm premenstrual. So I've chained myself to the
radiator.

— *Cynthia Heimel*

~ Snicker Doodles ~

These delicious cookies are covered in sugar and cinnamon, and when you bake them, the tops crackle to a sugary golden brown crisp. Sugar Plum Fairy Approved.

1½ cup sugar
½ cup butter, softened
½ cup shortening
2 eggs
2¾ cups flour
2 teaspoons cream of tartar
1 teaspoon baking soda
¼ teaspoon salt
3 tablespoons sugar
3½ teaspoons ground cinnamon

Preheat oven to 400°.

Mix 1½ cups sugar, butter, shortening, and eggs in a large bowl. Stir in flour, cream of tartar, baking soda, and salt until blended. Shape dough into teaspoon-sized balls.

Mix 3 tablespoons sugar and cinnamon; roll the balls in the cinnamon mixture. Place balls on cookie sheet, about 2 inches apart. Bake until set, about 8–10 minutes.

ALT: Any store-bought cinnamon cookies you can get your hands on, or make some cinnamon toast.

Male Tip: Give her the damn remote!

~ Pecan Pie ~

Sweet and Southern. Serve with a bottle of Southern Comfort or sarsaparilla.

4 eggs
1 cup brown sugar
1 cup light or dark corn syrup
½ teaspoon salt
¼ cup butter, melted
1 teaspoon vanilla
2 cups pecan halves
1 9-inch unbaked pie crust—don't bother making
  pie dough right now, ladies

Beat everything but pecans together well. Oh, what the hell, throw in another pinch of sugar. It is a sugar craving, after all. Stir in pecan halves. Pour mixture into pie crust and bake at 350° for 45–50 minutes, until set. Cool and eat with a big scoop of vanilla ice cream.

ALT: You can cram several of those little Bama Pecan Pies into your mouth at once.

Telltale PMS Symptom: You perspire like a construction worker and it's 20 below.

~ Raspberry Tart ~

If you're a sugar hound, this sweet raspberry tart is just for you. Guaranteed to give you a sugar rush and a great big smile (don't forget to pick the raspberry seeds out of your teeth).

4 cups fresh raspberries
1 cup sugar
⅓ cup Framboise (raspberry liqueur)
4 tablespoons cornstarch
1 tablespoon fresh lemon juice
⅛ teaspoon salt
unbaked pie or tart shell
2 tablespoons butter

Mix raspberries and sugar together lightly in bowl. *Lightly.* Whisk Framboise, cornstarch, lemon juice, and salt until smooth. Add that mixture to raspberry mixture and toss together. Pour into tart shell and dot with butter. Bake at 375° for 30 minutes, or until crust is golden brown.

ALT: Get those Scottish shortbread cookies and a pint of raspberries. Sip some Framboise or Chambord.

FUN FACT: G. J. Erdelyi studied female athletes and found some of them performed most poorly during the few days before they got their periods and the first two days of menstruation.

~ Pear and Apple Tarte Tatin ~

Nothing tastes better on a cold winter's day than hot apple pie. We've added pears and dressed up the old faithful. Don't forget the vanilla ice cream, whipped cream, or crème fraîche.

Pastry

1¼ cups unbleached flour
3 teaspoons sugar
¼ teaspoon salt
6 tablespoons butter, cut into small pieces, chilled
¼ cup ice water

Preheat oven to 400°.

In a food processor, fitted with a steel blade, blend flour, sugar, and salt. Add butter. Pulse until butter is the size of peas. Remove the lid and pour most of the water over the mixture. Pulse again; the dough should resemble curds and hold together. If not, add the rest of the water. Put dough between two sheets of wax paper. Roll out into a 10-inch circle. Chill for 2 hours.

Filling

Place in a bowl:

2 Bartlett pears, peeled, cored, and cut into quarters
2 Granny Smith apples, peeled, cored, and cut into quarters
juice of one lemon

In a 9-inch oven-proof skillet combine:

4 tablespoons butter
⅔ cup sugar

Cook butter and sugar over medium heat, stirring constantly, until mixture reaches a caramel color. Remove skillet from heat.

Add apples and pears to the skillet, arranging slices like a blossom, alternating pear with apple. Fill the center with remaining fruit.

Remove dough from fridge and peel away wax paper. Put the dough over the pears and apples on the skillet, tucking in the dough edges into the pan.

Bake until crust is golden brown (about 55 minutes). Let cool for 10 minutes. Invert tart onto a serving dish or eat right out of the pan.

ALT: Get a premade pie crust. Slice some pears and apples, sprinkle with lemon juice and sugar. Bake 50 minutes. Forget the fancy schmancy stuff. You want pie and you want it now.

Give me a dozen such heartbreaks, if that would help me lose a couple of pounds.

—Colette

~ Fritzi's Ex's Mother's Concord Grape Pie ~

Who ever heard of grape pie? None of us had until Fritzi had a bad case of PMS while she was visiting her ex-boyfriend's parents during grape-harvesting season. The only thing that kept the relationship together was the grape pie that was fed to Fritzi at regular intervals. Bake a few. It's the glue that'll hold your relationship together or make you think you still have a relationship.

If you're feeling edgy, throw some grapes into the tub and stomp away.

2 pounds concord grapes
1 tablespoon grated orange zest
1 tablespoon orange juice
1 tablespoon lemon juice
1 cup granulated sugar
2½ tablespoon quick-cooking tapioca
1 unbaked pastry for 2-crust 9-inch pie

Preheat oven to 425°.

Stem, rinse, and drain grapes. Schmush grapes between thumb and forefinger to slip skin from pulp. (Good way to get aggressions out.) Place skins in a bowl and pulp and seeds in sauce pan. Cook to boiling and then boil for one minute. Strain through a coarse sieve to remove seeds. Combine pulp with skins in the bowl. Stir in zest, orange juice, lemon juice, sugar, and tapioca. Allow to stand five minutes.

Fill pie with grape mixture. Cover with lattice or solid crust. Bake for 35–40 minutes. Serve with a quart of vanilla ice cream or whipped cream. Plan to eat the entire pie yourself.

ALT: Graham crackers and grape jelly mixed into the same quart of vanilla ice cream. Ben and Jerry would be proud.

MALE TIP: Stay out of the way.

~ *Cheesecake* ~

Simply the best cheesecake in the world. Simply. But not simple. At least not in your frame of mind. You can use half-the-fat cream cheese and sour cream if you like. Face it, you'll do no such thing. We like to eat the entire cheesecake. If you think someone else might want some, we recommend you bake two.

Crust

⅓ cup powdered sugar
1 stick butter
1½ cups graham cracker crumbs

Mix and pack firmly into 9-inch springform pan.

Filling

1 cup sugar
3 8-ounce packages of cream cheese
4 eggs
2 teaspoon vanilla

In a food processor, combine sugar, cream cheese, eggs, and vanilla. Process until smooth. Add mixture to crust.
Bake at 350° for 50 minutes.

Topping

1 pint sour cream
3 tablespoons sugar
½ teaspoon vanilla

In a separate bowl, combine sour cream, sugar, and vanilla. Mix until smooth. Spread on top of cheesecake. Return to oven for 5 minutes. Chill overnight.

ALT: Go to your local deli and order a cheesecake. Wait until you are safely inside your house to scarf it down. Or if you live in the middle of nowhere and can't get to a deli, remember, "Nobody does it like Sara Lee." As instructed above, eat the entire thing. Sure, you may feel sluggish, but you will know you have eaten an entire cheesecake. Like laundry, it's an accomplishment.

A woman without a man is like a fish without a bicycle.
—Gloria Steinem

~ Mexican Wedding Cake Cookies ~

Since you're in no condition to see ugly bridesmaid dresses, and the thought of two wonderfully happy, blissfully ecstatic people uniting will make you ill right now, we believe you can celebrate by yourself. So why not make these cookies and a rent a wedding video. We like *Muriel's Wedding* or the original *Father of the Bride*. We also recommend *Four Wedding and a Funeral,* but beware of the scene when Hugh Grant quotes David Cassidy.

1 cup butter
½ cup sugar
1 teaspoon vanilla
½ teaspoon salt
2 cups flour
1¼ cups walnuts, finely chopped (good to get out those frustrations)
Powdered sugar (for coating)

Combine butter, sugar, vanilla, and salt. Stir until smooth. Add flour and walnuts. Chill 10 minutes in refrigerator. Roll into tablespoon-sized balls. Bake at 350° for 15–20 minutes (bottoms should be hard). Roll in powdered sugar.

ALT: Get that blue-tinned butter cookie thing that you used to see collecting dust at your aunt's house. They're better if you smother them in powdered sugar. Eat as usual. Use the tin to bang on.

WARNING: If you have any small children, hide the tin after use. This will maintain a semblance of sanity and keep the officials from taking your kids away.

Never go to bed mad. Stay up and fight.
—*Phyllis Diller*

~ Peanut Butter Cookies ~

Most sharp instruments should be heavily guarded during this time. A fork is permitted, however, to make the criss-crosses on the cookies. Besides, it will give you the structure you've been looking for and an extra feeling of relief. Pretend you're Madonna and sing "Vogue" while performing. Then roll on the floor and wish on a lucky star. Fill your navel with peanut butter.

Cream in a bowl:

½ cup butter
½ cup chunky peanut butter
½ cup sugar
½ cup brown sugar
1 egg
1 teaspoon vanilla

In a separate bowl combine:

1¼ cups flour
½ teaspoon baking powder
½ teaspoon baking soda
¼ teaspoon salt
1 cup chocolate chips (optional)

Combine peanut butter mixture with flour mixture (and chocolate chips if you're using them). Chill for one hour.

Roll dough into 1-inch balls and use a fork to flatten with a crisscross pattern. Bake at 350° for 8–10 minutes.

ALT: Gaucho cookies are the best. Play with the creamy center.

It is sad to grow old, but nice to ripen.

—*Brigitte Bardot*

~ Lemon Squares ~

Because meringue is not something you want to be dealing with (separating eggs and worrying about the egg yolks falling into the egg whites is asking for catastrophe), we've included a good alternative to lemon meringue pie.

Besides, the lemon in these squares are a good match for the sour mood you're in.

In a bowl combine:

2 cups flour
½ cups confectioners sugar
1 cup melted butter

Pour into a 13 × 9 × 2-inch pan. Bake at 350° for 25 minutes.

Meanwhile, in a separate bowl combine:

1½ cups sugar
4 eggs
⅓ cup fresh lemon juice
zest of 1 lemon
½ teaspoon baking powder
¼ cup flour

Pour filling into baked crust. Bake for another 25 minutes. Cut into squares (if you feel like it) and dust with confectioners sugar.

ALT: Go to your local pie-theme restaurant and get a lemon meringue pie. Throw lemons at strangers. If you can't get to Marie Calendar's, suck on a lemon drop. Crunch it if you must, but we don't recommend it.

MALE TIP: Do not ask her to balance her checkbook right now.

~ Strawberry Shortcake ~

Strawberry shortcake, cream on top. And on the bottom. And in between. We like the cream all over. You may just want to make the cream and smother it all over your body. Sprinkle with strawberries and garnish with mint.

Strawberries

2 pints strawberries, cleaned and sliced
3 tablespoons fresh lemon juice
¼ cup sugar

Biscuits

1¾ cups all-purpose flour
1 tablespoon baking powder
¼ cup sugar
1 teaspoon salt
6 tablespoons cold, unsalted butter, cut into small pieces
¾ cup half and half or milk

Cream

whipping cream
1 teaspoon vanilla
2 tablespoons sugar

Preheat oven to 375°.

Combine strawberries, lemon juice, and ¼ cup sugar in a bowl, and set aside.

In another large bowl, combine flour, baking powder,

sugar, and salt. Using two knives, cut in butter until it resembles coarse meal. Add half and half or milk and mix with fork until dough comes together. Do not overmix.

Transfer dough to a lightly floured surface. Pat dough out to form a 6-inch square, ¾ inch thick. Cut 4 rounds using a 2½-inch cookie cutter. Place biscuits on cookie sheet. Bake 18 minutes, until golden brown.

While biscuits are baking, combine cream, vanilla, and sugar in a separate bowl. Whip until thick.

When biscuits are done, slice open and slather with strawberries and cream.

ALT: On a plate or in your hands, combine Pop in Fresh Country Biscuits, 2 cups thawed frozen strawberries, and 2 tablespoons sugar and Cool Whip.

Telltale PMS Symptom: Is that you or the Pillsbury Dough Boy?

~ Rice Krispies Treats ~

If you're about to snap, crackle, or pop, these might take the edge off. And did you know marshmallows are almost 100% sugar?

¼ cup butter
1 10-ounce package large marshmallows or 4 cups
miniature marshmallows
6 cups Kellogg's Rice Krispies

Melt butter with marshmallows. Add Rice Krispies. Stir. Using buttered spatula or waxed paper, press mixture evenly into buttered 13 × 9 × 2-inch pan. Cut into 2-inch squares or eat in its entirety.

ALT: Take a spoon of Fluff and pour Rice Krispies on top.

MALE TIP: Do not channel-surf.

4

THE SALT FIX

~ ~ ~ ~ ~

Lee's Artichoke Dip
Oriental Spaghetti
Dorothy's Potato Pancakes
Janet's Spinach Dip
Stir Fry
Skirt Steak
Huevos Rancheros
Pizza
Jen's Caesar Salad
Hot Crab Dip
Guacamole
3–2–1 Margarita

~ ~ ~

Old salt. Salt of the earth. Salty dog. Salt fix. Don't divorce the salt and pepper. Saltwater taffy. Salty seas. Salt N Pepa . . . When PMS hits, some of us crave salty chips and nuts, high-sodium Chinese food, and most importantly during this time, salty margaritas. Sometimes the craving is so strong that only an old-fashioned farm salt lick will really do the trick. But hanging out with a bunch of cows isn't nearly as fun as eating the delicious salty favorites in this chapter. If you'd rather have an anchovy pizza than a piece of cake, this chapter is for you.

So you're craving salt. What perfect timing, considering the fact that salt can only aggravate the water bloat that comes with PMS. So why not go for broke? As Mom always says, if it's worth doing at all, it's worth doing well. So prepare for the big bloat. Put those sexy jeans in the back of your closet and bring out the baggy drawstring sweats. Don't even think about checking out your rearview in a G-string right now, ladies. But you've got an excuse for that all-over puffiness, at least for a week. So rent a mushy movie, sit back with some salty popcorn, pretzels, chips, and a salt 'n' lime tequila and cry some salty tears for the heartbroken heroine on the screen. After all . . . better her than you.

~ Lee's Artichoke Dip ~

A calorie extravaganza. Fast. Easy. To the point. Our friend Lee loves to make this for all our parties. Why share? There are enough calories in this dish to last you a couple of days. Remember, this is just a snack. We recommend you sample other recipes before calling it a day.

2 small cans cut-up green chilis
2 cans artichokes, quartered
2 packages frozen spinach, thawed and drained
1½ –2 cups mayonnaise (the more the creamier)
1–1½ cups Parmesan cheese (the more the better)

Mix all these ingredients and throw in a 9 × 13 × 2-inch pan. Bake at 450°–500° for 20 minutes. Eat with the large, huge, extra-big Fritos.

ALT: Dip the same Fritos in a jar of mayonnaise. Same calorie effect.

"No French woman would attempt to make a mayonnaise sauce while in that state."

—*Briffault*

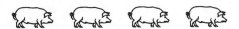

~ Oriental Spaghetti ~

Tastes like the real thing. Make extra sauce because you might want it. Actually, doubling, tripling, quadrupling (etc.) the recipe is easy and allows for more consumption. And Chinese food is famous for its sodium content.

Get some chopsticks. Then again, that may aggravate you. Forget the chopsticks. Use your hands.

¼ cup peanut butter
1 tablespoon soy sauce
1 tablespoon lemon juice
1 small garlic clove, minced
¼ teaspoon dried hot pepper
¼ cup hot water
¼ teaspoon sugar
6 ounces spaghetti cooked spaghetti
1 cucumber, peeled, seeded, and cut diagonally into
   ⅛-inch slices
⅓ cup scallions

In a blender, combine peanut butter, soy sauce, lemon juice, garlic, pepper flakes, sugar, and hot water, until smooth. In a large bowl combine peanut butter sauce with cooked spaghetti. Add cucumber slices and scallions.

ALT: Call your local Chinese restaurant and order their sesame noodles. Have them throw in some spare ribs for that gnawing, chewing feel.

MALE TIP: Don't be chipper.

~ Dorothy's Potato Pancakes ~

Mom made these when she wanted to nurture us. And they worked. Try them yourself. As Fritzi's mom says: "Don't put any extra crap in your potato pancakes." And they're salty enough to satisfy your craving.

4 potatoes—2 shredded finely, 2 shredded coarsely (press out extra liquid)
1 egg
1 medium onion, shredded finely
salt and pepper to taste

Combine all ingredients. Heat butter in a large skillet. Spoon mixture into 3-inch patties. Cook until golden brown on bottom, turn, and brown the other side.

Serve with applesauce, sour cream, ketchup, yogurt, peanut butter, and anything else that makes you happy (any extra "crap" you think of). They're *your* pancakes, after all. No one is watching (not even Fritzi's mom). Far be it from us to tell you what to put in or on your potato pancakes.

ALT: Head out to Arby's for a potato pancake and smother it with Arby's Horsy sauce. Or Ore-Ida hash browns. Or Tater Tots.

MALE TIP: Do not say "You're just premenstrual." She'll deny it and throw you out of the house. A good reason to throw things at you as well.

~ Janet's Spinach Dip ~

Our friend Janet introduced this dip to us, but it's an old party favorite. Some people put the dip in a hollowed-out bread. We feel this is an added step, not necessary and a little too cute for the mood you're in. There should be enough salt in the leek soup mix to satisfy your sodium search.

WARNING: There could be a problem waiting for the spinach to thaw. Make sure your microwave is working or be prepared to wait. Canned spinach works also.

1 box frozen spinach, thawed and drained
¾ box leek soup mix
1 cup mayonnaise
16 ounces sour cream
⅔ cup parsley, minced
1 teaspoon dill
1 bunch scallions, chopped

Combine all ingredients. Eat with vegetables if you want. We prefer chips, crackers . . . anything with a higher fat content.

ALT: Leftover onion dip. Add spinach.

FUN FACT: In 1921 the first disposable sanitary napkin was introduced. Tampons were introduced to the American market in the mid-1930s by Tampax.

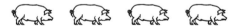

~ Stir Fry ~

There will be a mess in your kitchen. Call in professional help. All kinds. All for you. Cleaning women, psychiatrists, chefs, butlers, baby-sitters. Have the sitter read you a bedtime story.

½ cup peanut oil
1 pound tofu and/or chicken breasts, cut into strips
1 ounce shittake mushrooms, soaked in boiling
    water for 30 minutes, then sliced (reserve
    liquid for sauce)

Any of the following (or what's in your fridge):

1 red pepper, julienne   **1 can baby corn,**
1 bunch scallions   **drained**
1 head bok choy,   **1 can water chestnuts,**
    cleaned and chopped   **drained and thinly**
½ pound snow peas   **sliced**
2 celery sticks, julienne   **1 pound mung beans**
2 carrots, gallant

Sauce

liquid reserved from soaking mushrooms
1½ tablespoons minced fresh ginger
5 cloves garlic, minced
3 tablespoons dry sherry
2 tablespoons soy sauce
chili oil

In a very hot wok (or skillet), add ¼ cup peanut oil. Then add chicken and/or tofu and sauté until just cooked. Remove chicken/tofu from wok and put on a plate.

Add remaining ¼ cup oil to wok, throw in mushrooms and the vegetables you've chosen, and stir fry. Remove from wok and add them to the chicken/tofu plate.

Put reserved mushroom-soaking liquid, ginger, garlic, sherry, soy sauce, and a dash of chili oil into wok and cook for 1 minute, until thickened. Add chicken/tofu and vegetables to wok and mix well.

Serve with rice, if you like. (You can figure that out, or pay a visit to Uncle Ben.)

ALT: Get a sauce pan. Throw in some frozen vegetables. Add some salad dressing. Consume. If some of the vegetables are still frozen, that's okay. Unless this annoys you.

FUN FACT: Japanese women reported fewer premenstrual symptoms than Turkish, Nigerian, and American women.

~ Skirt Steak ~

Meat has a lot of iron and it also has a wonderfully salty flavor. Usually around PMS time, the cravings for meat come up. We've included our favorite steak. Serve it rare.

4 6-ounce skirt steaks

Marinade

   ¼ **cup red wine**
   2 tablespoons soy sauce
   2 tablespoons balsamic vinegar
   2 minced garlic cloves
   2 tablespoons chopped cilantro
   1 teaspoon sugar
   ¼ **teaspoon white pepper**
   ⅓ **cup olive oil**

Put all the ingredients except the oil in a blender. Then, with the blender on, add the oil in a slow steady stream.

Marinate the steaks at least 5 hours, or overnight if possible (or don't even bother, 'cause you're hungry).

Grill the steaks or cook them under a broiler. For medium rare: 3–4 minutes on each side.

ALT: Forget the marinade. Get a filet mignon. Broil it. Eat it. Oooh la la. Serve with a bottle of your favorite red. Or toaster steaks?

"Cleaning your house while your kids are still growing is like shoveling the walk before it stops snowing."

—*Phyllis Diller*

~ Huevos Rancheros ~

Hey, chica. Feeling adventurous? How's about a trip to Mexico this morning? 'Cause we're making eggs, Mexican style. If the Incas and the Aztecs could do it, so can you. Paint a warrior mask on your face with some of the ingredients and attack.

Songs to sing while assembling ingredients: "Vamos a la Playa," "Feliz Navidad," or "La Cucaracha." But any ethnic song you don't know the full meaning of will do.

oil for frying
2 tortillas
1 batch of refried beans (black or pinto)
grated cheese
2 eggs over easy
1 batch guacamole (*see* recipe, p. 98)
1 batch salsa
sour cream

Fry tortillas in a sauce pan until lightly golden on both sides. Bake tortillas with beans and cheese 4–6 minutes. Fry your eggs. Place eggs on baked beans and cheese. Top with guacamole and salsa and sour cream.

ALT: Get serious. You're either gonna do this or you're not.

One is not born a woman, one becomes one.
                                    —*Simone de Beauvoir*

~ Pizza ~

Ciao bella! Pizza is not only delicious, but also deliciously salty. Especially if you add anchovies and olives. But you're in no condition to make pizza dough. Much less make the sauce, grate the cheese—you get the picture. We have given you four ALTS:

1. Order in. Check your yellow pages under "Pizza."

2. Purchase the following:

   1½ Boboli pizza crust
   1½ Ragu sauce (or any other to your liking)
   1½ pregrated cheese

and any of the following toppings:

anchovies	**onion**
artichoke hearts	**pepperoni**
basil leaves	**pesto**
1½ capers	**pine nuts**
1½ chicken	**roasted pepper**
(barbecued)	**salsa**
cilantro	**sausage**
garlic	**shrimp**
goat cheese	**sun-dried tomatoes**
olives	**zucchini**

Throw in the oven at 450° for 10–12 minutes.

3. English muffin pizza or french bread pizza

1 English muffin or French bread
some red sauce
some mozzarella cheese

Toast the English muffin. Put some sauce on it and some cheese. Pop in toaster oven or broiler for 3 minutes.

4. Frozen pizza. We like Wolfgang Puck's for its variety and flavor challenge.

MALE TIP: Don't invite your mother to stay for the weekend.

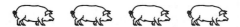

~ Jen's Caesar Salad ~

One of the saltiest foods you can eat, not only because of the traditional anchovy, but also because of the secret added ingredient: capers. Add some salty herbed croutons to this salad and prepare for ecstasy, salt fiends.

Smash in a bowl:

3–4 cloves garlic
1 teaspoon anchovy paste
dash salt

Add:

1 tablespoon capers, also crushed (all the crushing and smashing will do you good)

Then add:

1 tablespoon Worcestershire sauce
⅓ –½ cup oil
1 tablespoon lemon juice
1 tablespoon mayonnaise
¼ cup balsamic vinegar
1 teaspoon Dijon

Beat it up until mixture is creamy.
Toss on **1 head of romaine lettuce** with:

Parmesan cheese
croutons

Enjoy with a hunk of salty bread and a glass of white wine. Only God knows how much sodium is in this meal.

ALT: Bag of prepared salad and Newman's Own Caesar Dressing. Add salt.

Telltale PMS Symptom: You think you may explode at any moment.

~ Hot Crab Dip ~

Feeling crabby? Hah. We've got just the dip. Treat yourself. You will eat the entire thing. You can add salt, but the crabmeat may have just enough.

3 ounces cream cheese, softened
½ cup mayonnaise
1 6-ounce can crabmeat, drained
¼ cup minced onion
1 tablespoon lemon juice
⅛ teaspoon Tabasco sauce

In an oven-proof dish, beat cream cheese until smooth. Add remaining ingredients. Bake at 350° for 30 minutes, or until bubbly.

ALT: 1 cup sour cream, 1 package of Lipton Onion Recipe Soup Mix. Pretend there's crab in it and that it's hot.

"I've been sort of crabby lately. It's that time of the month again—the rent is due."

—*Margaret Smith*

~ *Guacamole* ~

Is there anything in this world better for a salt fiend than a big bowl of delicious guacamole with a handful (yeah, right, *one* handful) of salty tortilla chips? And remember, although avocados have 40 grams of fat each *(aaahhhhh!!)*, it's *vegetable* fat, which is much easier for your body to break down than *animal* fat (i.e., lard). Avocados are also rich in vitamin E, which does amazing things for your skin, so go to town. Rationalize, rationalize, rationalize. Just be sure to wipe the green stuff off your mouth before you kiss your significant other.

1 ripe Haas avocado (or more, depending on craving)
¼ cup sour cream (like there wasn't enough fat already)
¼ cup salsa of your choice (or more, to taste)
handful of fresh cilantro
juice of ½ lime
1 jalapeño, chopped
1 teaspoon chopped onion

Mash avocado in a bowl. Add sour cream, salsa, chopped cilantro, lime juice, jalapeño, and onion. Mush the mixture up really well until it resembles something you'd want to eat. Add more of whatever you want to suit your taste buds.

Dip huge white corn tortilla chips into it (you can also squeeze lime juice on chips for an extra kick) and crunch away your blues with this creamy, obscenely fattening delicacy.

Think wrongly, if you please, but in all cases think for yourself.

—*Doris Lessing*

~ 3-2-1 Margarita ~

3–2–1: Countdown to sanity with this salty, delicious beverage. Great with any of the Mexican dishes in this book, with chips, or on its own. We guarantee this margarita will not only soothe your nerves, but also satisfy even the most intense salt craving.

3 shots tequila
2 shots lime juice
1 shot triple sec

Mix. (Blender and ice are optional.) Pour into chilled, salted glasses. Share with a couple of friends.

TIP: Do not attempt to drive or operate heavy machinery after drinking this. But then you have PMS—you shouldn't be doing these things anyway.

Telltale PMS Symptom: You buy things you don't want, need, or like.

5

CASSEROLES AND CONCOCTIONS

~ ~ ~ ~ ~ ~

Chuckwagon Skillet
Dottie's Green Bean Casserole
Frito Pie
Veggie Gratin
Broccoli Cheese Casserole
Cassoulet
Chips 'n' Beans
Tuna Casserole
Potato Chip Sandwich
Tomato Sandwich
Peanut Butter and Onion Sandwich
Banana and Peanut Butter Sandwich
Fluffer Nutter Sandwich
Peanut Butter and Bacon Sandwich

(continued)

Elvis's Potato Sandwich
Fried Bologna Sandwich
Bread, Butter, and Sugar Sandwich
Fritzi and Julie's English Muffin and Melted
Muenster
Ambrosia
Julie's Sour Cream and Walnuts Delight
Sugar and Pecans
Four-Can Deep Tuna Pie
Kira's Cosmic Chile con Queso
T-Town Queso
Diane's Curry Parmesan Popcorn
Heavenly Banana Split
The Salt/Sugar Thing

~ ~ ~

If it's warm, big, and baked, you'll find it in this chapter. And if it's weird, different, yet essential in a PMS moment, you'll also find it in this chapter. Casseroles and concoctions: sometimes the same, sometimes very different. Casseroles usually have noodles or some creamy soup product added to them. Concoctions are usually whatever you come up with in the privacy of your own kitchen.

What role casseroles play for the woman with PMS is clear—they are the perfect entrée for someone who isn't thinking with a clear head. In the classic state of PMS frustration and confusion, you can simply toss several ingredients into an ovenproof dish, shove it in the oven, and sprawl yourself nearby with a bottle of gin until the timer awakens you. You can feed your family well while at the same time give off a clear signal to your husband and children: When they see casserole, they know better than to bother Mommy. There are leftovers in case you can't get out of bed the next day, and there is only one large dish to clean or let soak in the sink for a week, by which time PMS symptoms will disappear. In this chapter, we have combined the best of our old-time favorite casseroles along with a few unique new casseroles that are delightful enough to serve at a dinner party.

But what about concoctions? Any PMS sufferer knows that concoctions are the foundation of PMS eating. Random, crazy, and creative concoctions serve to satisfy a food urge immediately. So what's in the fridge? Pickles, sauerkraut, mustard, and rice cakes? Sounds like a concoction to us. Peanut butter, chocolate syrup, bee pollen, and roasted almonds? How about some avocado on top of that? Yep. Concoction. You get the idea. Make up your own. Write them down and keep a record of the marvels you come up with. So when you're feeling too harried to make separate dishes for dinner, turn the page and prepare to concoct a masterpiece, whether it be a delicious casserole or a courageous concoction.

CASSEROLES
~ Chuckwagon Skillet ~

Yeehaw! Straight out of Texas in the fifties, here is a casserole your family can't live without.

½ **cup onion**
1 **cup celery, chopped**
2 **tablespoons butter**
1 **pound ground beef**
1 **teaspoon salt**
1 **teaspoon pepper**
1 **can stewed tomatoes**
½ **cup water**
2 **cups pasta noodles of your choice**
2 **cups shredded cheddar cheese**

Sauté onion and celery in butter. Take this opportunity to cry—just let it all out. Okay. Now, add meat, salt, and pepper. Brown meat. Pour tomatoes and water in. Simmer 25 minutes. Cook noodles. Mix everything together. You can eat it like that or top with cheese, or bake it at 350° for 10 minutes.

It seems as if the only suitable wine for this would be Boone's, or you could just drink a tall glass of ice cold milk. Welcome to the Heartland

ALT: Open a can of Heinz Sloppy Joes. Pour over anything with carbohydrates: potatoes, pasta, bread, your kids.

Ask your child what he wants for dinner only if he's buying.

—*Fran Lebowitz*

~ Dottie's Green Bean Casserole ~

Ah yes, Mom's staple at every holiday dinner. The joys of those little canned French-fried onions cannot be underestimated. And no casserole chapter would be right without them. Read on and see why.

1 quart canned green beans
1 can cream of mushroom soup
salt and pepper
¼ cup of milk
1 can French-fried onion rings

Mix everything up in whatever order you want. Bake at 350° for 15 minutes. Eat it up.

ALT: Open a can of green beans, heat 'em, and eat 'em.

MALE TIP: Refrain from chuckling to yourself for no reason.

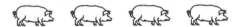

~ Frito Pie ~

If you've ever wondered how you gained "the Freshman 15" pounds during college, Frito Pie may be your answer. Gobbled up in the wee hours of the morning with your best friends after a night of frat parties (where you demurely nibbled on carrot sticks in front of your date), this is truly an American concoction, and is a nostalgic craving for many PMS sufferers. Not only is it packed with calories, but the Fritos provide the crunching sensation that is so satisfying to us at this time.

1 bag Fritos (you determine the size)
1 can of Texas chili (Aha! *This* is what canned
**   Hormel's is for!)**
½ cup shredded cheddar cheese

Pour the chips into a bowl. Heat the chili and pour over chips. Top with shredded cheese and let it melt all over the chili. If you don't feel like doing dishes, you can just leave the chips in the Frito bag, split it open, and repeat the above (aka "Bruce's Chili Boo," named after our friend Bruce, who is too lazy to get up and get a plate). Guaranteed to make you feel like a teenager again!

ALT: Chili-flavored Fritos.

MALE TIP: Pretend it's Christmas and she is the Lord. Be a wise man. Bear gifts.

~ *Veggie Gratin* ~

Yes, even vegetarians need casseroles and concoctions when they've got PMS, and this dish is so delicious, you carnivorous ladies may never head for the hamburger stand again.

½ onion, chopped
2 teaspoons butter (or more if you're really
    indulging)
1 cup mushrooms, sliced
1 cup carrots, chopped or cubed
2 potatoes, sliced
½ cup broccoli
⅛ cup milk or cream
½ cup Gruyère cheese

Sauté onion in butter until soft. Add veggies and toss with butter/onion mixture. Put entire mixture in medium-sized casserole dish. Add milk, dot with butter, cover with Gruyère cheese, and bake at 350° for about 30–45 minutes until cheese is golden brown and veggies are soft. Eat with some really good bread and a glass of dry red wine. This dish just can't be beat to cure the PMS blues.

ALT: A bag of frozen vegetables and a hunk of Velveeta. Microwave. Eat while watching television. You'll miss that weird flavor.

FUN FACT: As to New England ax murderer Lizzie Bor-den, evidence suggests that these famous murders took place during the time of her period (Marcia Storch, How to Relieve Cramps).

~ Broccoli Cheese Casserole ~

Forget steamed broccoli, girls. Here's a casserole that gives you license to smother one of Mother Nature's healthiest veggies in creamy, delicious CHEESE.

**2–3 cups fresh broccoli heads, chopped and
  steamed
1 cup cooked rice
1 small onion, chopped
1 tablespoon butter
½ pound Velveeta cheese (seriously)
½ cup milk
1 can cream of mushroom soup
1 can cream of chicken soup
handful of slivered almonds (optional)**

Stir together steamed broccoli and rice. Sauté onion in butter until soft. Add to rice mixture. Cook cheese, milk, and soups all together in saucepan over medium heat. Mix together with broccoli/rice mixture, and put in casserole dish. Top with slivered almonds. Bake 35–40 minutes at 350°. This serves eight to ten normal people, so you should get two premenstrual servings for yourself. Grab a spatula and dig right in.

ALT: Toss a few frozen broccoli pieces into a bowl, top with cheddar cheese, and microwave until cheese melts. NOTE: If you do not wait for it to cool, you will burn your tongue.

A man has to be Joe McCarthy to be called ruthless. All a woman has to do is put you on hold.

—*Marlo Thomas*

~ Cassoulet ~

Yes, even chic French women get PMS. It's just that when they complain, it still sounds so fabulous with that accent. Sure, with those svelte figures, they may bypass the Desperado Feasts, but our sources tell us that they often go straight for the cassoulet, a casserole of duck and beans that is just loaded with salt and fat. A nice big bottle of Beaujolais is a must with this delectable dish, and of course, that's just your portion. *Bon appétit!*

4 pieces bacon, chopped
2 pounds boneless shoulder or leg of lamb, cut into pieces
1 pound smoked breast of duck
1 tablespoon flour
4 cups chicken or beef stock (get Swanson's in a can)
1 teaspoon salt
Ground fresh pepper (½ teaspoon or more)
2 teaspoons fines herbes
2 garlic cloves, chopped
2 tablespoons tomato paste
1 16 oz can northern beans
½ cup breadcrumbs
4 tablespoons chopped parsley

Sauté bacon and meat together until well browned. Transfer meat to casserole dish. Sprinkle flour over it and pour in broth. Season with salt, pepper, and herbs. Add garlic and tomato paste. Add beans to meat mixture. Sprinkle with breadcrumbs and parsley and bake at 400° for 30 minutes or until well browned on top. Prepare to look like a tubby French peasant (a *happy,* tubby, French peasant).

ALT: Van Camp's Beanee Weanees, right out of the can.

If you obey all the rules, you miss all the fun.
                                        —*Katharine Hepburn*

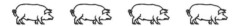

~ Chips 'n' Beans ~

If you happen to be at a barbecue the next time you've got PMS, you're in luck! Just grab a handful of potato chips and a bowl of barbecue beans, and dip to your heart's content. This is an ideal PMS concoction because it satisfies both the salt and sugar craving at the same time. In case it isn't the barbecue season when you've got the craving, we've provided the following recipe for your dipping pleasure.

¼ cup onion, chopped
2 medium cans pork 'n' beans
⅓ cup brown sugar (or more, if you've got a sweet tooth)
¼ cup ketchup

Put all ingredients in a casserole and bake at 350° for 30–45 minutes. Get a big bag of Ruffles. Dip into beans.

ALT: Pop-top can of pork 'n' beans. Bag of chips.

MALE TIP: Do not click your tongue, smack your lips, or crack your knuckles if you value your life.

~ Tuna Casserole ~

This brings back those old days when Mom did the cooking and we didn't know any better. Take yourself back to the days when you didn't have PMS. Just acne and funny looks from the boy next door and years of school ahead of you. Things could be worse. That's right, they are. PMS. Sorry to gnat you. Back to the food. Creamy and delicious. Dive into the warm, soothing, yummy casserole. We'll meet you there.

We like to double the bread crumb mixture.

2 cups cooked noodles, egg or fusilli or what's in the cabinet
1 6-ounce can tuna, drained and flaked
1 can cream of mushroom soup
Optional: 1 cup frozen peas (this may scare some of you)

Put all ingredients into a buttered 1½-quart casserole dish and bake at 400° for 25 minutes.

Topping:

1 tablespoon butter
3 tablespoons dry bread crumbs

In a saucepan, melt the butter and add crumbs, browning them. Sprinkle on top of casserole. Serve it up.

Instead of the bread crumbs, use potato chips.

ALT: Stouffer's Tuna Noodle Casserole.

Telltale PMS Symptom: Your nipples feel as if they weigh 20 pounds.

CONCOCTIONS

All of the following will make fabulous tea sandwiches.

~ Potato Chip Sandwich ~

2 pieces bread   **potato chips**
mayonnaise

You get the crunch, you get the salt, and you get the comfortable feeling of soft, mushy bread.

~ Tomato Sandwich ~

2 pieces bread   **tomato slices**
mayonnaise   **salt**

We like lots of salt on these.

~ Peanut Butter and Onion Sandwich ~

2 pieces of bread   **peanut butter**
onion slices

The comfort of peanut butter and the bad breath of the onion will make you feel better while keeping those annoying humans away.

~ Banana and Peanut Butter Sandwich ~

2 pieces bread   **one mushed banana**
peanut butter

An old lunch-box favorite. Serve with a cold glass of milk and an apple for your teacher.

VARIATION: Add one tablespoon of butter to a skillet and sauté the sandwich on both sides.

~ Fluffer Nutter Sandwich ~

2 pieces bread   **Marshmallow Fluff**
peanut butter

This may stick to the roof of your mouth.

~ Peanut Butter and Bacon Sandwich ~

2 pieces bread   **2 teaspoons**
¼ cup peanut butter   **Worcestershire**
2 strips bacon   **sauce**
                             2 teaspoon mince
                             onion

Call us strange, but this sandwich has the power to inspire and awe.

"What you eat standing up doesn't count."
                                        —*Beth Barnes*

~ Elvis's Potato Sandwich ~

2 pieces bread
½ pound bacon,
   browned (reserve
   drippings)
sliced onions

2 potatoes, sliced ¼
   inch thick
mustard or ketchup

Okay, Elvis didn't have PMS, but what were those weird jumpsuits all about?

Fry onions and potatoes in bacon fat until potatoes are cooked, about 10 minutes. Slap some mustard or ketchup on the bread, and layer with bacon, onion, and potatoes.

Mmmmm . . . greasy and good.

~ Fried Bologna Sandwich ~

2 pieces bread
2 slices bologna

mustard (optional)

Greasy, gross, and glutinous.

Throw the bologna in a skillet, fry on both sides. Put on bread—don't forget to put the grease from the skillet on the bread.

~ Bread, Butter, and Sugar Sandwich ~

2 pieces bread   **sugar to cover bread**
¼ stick of butter,
   softened

Sound weird? It's really good.

~ Fritzi and Julie's English Muffin and Melted Muenster ~

Fritzi and her friend Julie used to eat these right after the sour cream and walnut delight. (See "Julie's Sour Cream and Walnuts Delight," p. 125.) Followed by a bowl of corn flakes.

Toast an English muffin. Smother with two slices of muenster cheese. Melt in toaster oven or in oven broiler until melted.

~ Untitled 101 ~

Sourdough, avocado, and sesame seeds. (Mayo and soy sauce are optional.)

~ Untitled 102 ~

Tuna and potato chip sandwich.

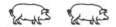

~ Untitled 103 ~

Butter sandwich. Get the creamiest, best butter you can find and lay it on thick.

~ Untitled 104 ~

Chocolate chip toast sandwich. Spread butter and chocolate chips on warm toast. The chocolate chips will get all melted and gooey. Mmmm.

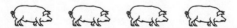

~ Untitled 105 ~

Buffalo wings with ranch or blue cheese dressing.

~ Untitled 106 ~

Apple wedges with honey, caramel, or peanut butter.

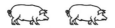

~ Lynn's PMS Combo ~

Our friend Lynn insists that a grilled cheese sandwich (slap one slice American cheese between two slices toasted white bread) and a chocolate milkshake (*see* Chapter 7, "Cramping Your Style") are the only way to go. If you can't manage that, she recommends tuna, straight out of the can.

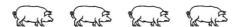

~ Ambrosia ~

An old favorite. If this dish has too many memories, don't make it.

2 large oranges, peeled and sliced, or canned mandarin oranges

3 ripe bananas, sliced

1½ cups shredded coconut

¼ cup confectioners sugar

Mix well. Chill well before eating.

Optional Additions:

1 8-ounce can chopped pineapple with juice

1 cup sour cream or Cool Whip

ALT: Mush some coconut into a can of Libby's Fruit Cocktail. *See* "Optional Additions."

~ Julie's Sour Cream and Walnuts Delight ~

Julie turned Fritzi on to this concoction after school during their first bouts of PMS. Fast and easy. You can eat it right out of the container.

¼ cup sour cream   **1 banana (optional)**
½ cup walnuts

~ Sugar And Pecans ~

Just that. In a bowl.

MALE TIP: Figure out what you're doing that annoys her and don't do it.

~ Four-Can Deep Tuna Pie ~

All you need is a can opener and a casserole dish. What could be simpler? Drinking milk from the carton or, perhaps, watching infomercials.

1 can Campbell's mushroom soup
1 4 ounce can evaporated milk
1 can French-style green beans, drained

1 6-ounce can tuna
1 box frozen onion rings

In a 1½-quart casserole dish, mix soup with milk. Add beans and tuna. Bake at 400° for 20 minutes. Top with onion rings. Bake another 10 minutes.

ALT: Open a can of tuna. Open your mouth. Dump it in. Of course, this just screams for a fruity Chardonnay.

~ Kira's Cosmic Chile con Queso ~

Our buddy Kira makes this disgusting, delicious, globby mass of processed cheese for parties and during her bouts of PMS. She swears it takes her cramps away. "If you eat it, your arteries clog, so your body stops cramping and kicks into survival mode." As Kira reminds us: "This is basically melted Velveeta. Yum."

1 box Velveeta, diced
½ to 1 cup milk, as
 needed
bag of Fritos

either 1 jar picante
 sauce or 1 can
 peeled tomatoes and
 chile

Throw cheese in a crockpot or saucepan over medium heat, stirring occasionally. As cheese melts, gradually add milk. Continue to stir to avoid burning the cheese. (This will annoy you.) After cheese and milk have melted smooth, add picante sauce or tomatoes. Stir. Dip Fritos. Wash down with ice-cold Cerveza.

Kira suggests you keep this in a heated pot to avoid coagulation.

~ T-Town Queso ~

This is the way Jen remembers this stuff, which is a staple in every teenager's diet back home in Tulsa, Oklahoma. Jen doesn't mind admitting that it is still one of her favorites. How can Velveeta taste so good? Go figure.

Velveeta
1 can stewed tomatoes

Optional: 1 can chili (for the really brave of heart)

Stick hunk of Velveeta and contents of Rotel (and chili, if using it) in the microwave in a big bowl and hit HIGH. Watch it bubble. Stir it up. Dip salty tortilla chips in. Ahhhh.

~ Diane's Curry Parmesan Popcorn ~

Microwave one of those bags of popcorn. Throw on some more butter, Parmesan cheese, and curry powder. Our pal Diane says: "This provides a valuable source of salt and fat."

I finally figured out that the only reason to be alive is to enjoy it.

—*Rita Mae Brown*

~ Heavenly Banana Split ~

A PMS standard. We've improved the soda fountain original. Be creative and explore all the possibilities.

1 chocolate-covered banana
3 scoops of your favorite ice cream (we like a scoop each of Ben and Jerry's Chunky Monkey, Coffee Toffee Crunch, and Chubby Hubby)

toppings
whipped Cream

Apply liberal amounts of chocolate fudge, butterscotch sauce, and caramel sauce. Top with chunks and crumbs made from Oreos, brownies, chocolate chip cookies, Heathbars, Butterfingers, M&M's, nuts, and chocolate chips. Slather with fresh whipped cream. A cherry on top if you're the old-fashioned type.

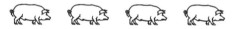

~ The Salt/Sugar Thing ~

Sometimes we like to have our sugar with our salt. Or our salt with our sugar. Here are some combinations that work really well:

Ketchup and eggs
Scrambled eggs and jam
Popcorn and:
    Milkduds
    Gummi Bears
    Raisinettes
    Chocolate chips
    M&M's
    Snowcaps
    Hershey's Kisses (especially with almonds)
    Hershey's Hugs (white chocolate)
English muffin with butter *and* jam
Pretzels and chocolate
Sausage or bacon with maple syrup
Indian food, e.g., curry with mango chutney
Caramel popcorn or Cracker Jacks
Chocolate-covered saltines
Sweet and sour pork with soy sauce
Peanut brittle
Potato chips and ketchup. Wash down with huge bottle of Pepsi.
Bread and chocolate
Ham or lamb and mint jelly
Duck à l'orange
Jelly beans and Triscuits
Egg salad on raisin toast
Foie gras on raisin toast

Salty rosemary bread with jelly
Turkey and cranberry sauce (also great as a sandwich)

MALE TIP: Remember the Golden Rule: She's right and you're wrong. Accept it.

6

DESPERADO
FEASTS

~ ~ ~ ~ ~ ~

Denial Feasting
The Bed Picnic
The Public Pig-Out
The Sweet Feast
Hurl and Rage

~ ~ ~

Feast or famine . . . ? The answer at this time of the month is definitely FEAST. We believe in feasting like the Royalty (or beasts, in some cases) that we are. And since we're all desperados when we have PMS, the sky is the limit. In this chapter, we give you some of our favorite desperado feasts and believe that, although you may not want to admit it, you'll recognize these wild, no-holds-barred eating binges. So open your fridge or dash off to your market, and prepare to indulge in some of the most incredible feasts divined since ancient times.

NOTE: All desperado feasts have a 4-pig rating.

Denial Feasting

You don't want to admit you're pigging out (to yourself or anyone else), but every chance you get, massive amounts of food float into your mouth. Cook a feast for your significant other, then eat seconds and scrape his plate clean in the privacy of your kitchen. Have temper tantrum when he doesn't immediately offer to do the dishes.

Sample Menu 1: The Russian. Cook too much chicken Kiev, insist he take three helpings, then pop the two he doesn't eat into your mouth while cleaning up.

Sample Menu 2: The Scavenger. Pick at your cheese fries, stroganoff, and chocolate mousse while at the table; sniffle and moan every once in a while so he'll feel sorry for you. Notice what he's not eating and plan for your attack when he's not looking. Open your eyes really big, like a puppy dog, and tell him you don't mind the pain. Then eat whatever is on his plate, i.e., bread scraps, crumbs, garnishes.

Denial Feasting Tips:
> Crumbs don't count calorie-wise.
> Eating upside down helps digestion.
> Eat standing up; gravity helps.
> Talk on the phone or watch TV—forget what you're eating.
> No matter what, remember: None of this pigging out has anything to do with a hormonal imbalance or PMS.

Life itself is the proper binge.

—Julia Child

The Bed Picnic

Rent a movie, prepare a feast, spread a beach towel on the bed. Spread the entire feast on the bed and eat while watching the movie. All those calories without ever having to leave the comfort of your bed. Brush the crumbs away and doze off.

Sample Menu 1: The European. Wine, various types of cheeses, particularly triple cremes such as St. André (if not available, Brie and Camembert will do); pâté de foie gras, vegetable pâté, French bread, Italian focaccia, Belgian chocolates . . . You get the idea. (Movie choices: *Babette's Feast, Like Water for Chocolate,* or *Eat Drink Man Woman.*)

Sample Menu 2: The South American. Nachos with extra scoops of guacamole (*see* p. 98) and sour cream, Mongo Burrito (*see* p. 46), miniquesadillas, taquitos, and of course, margaritas or Coronas with lime. Play Latin music and dance with a rose in your mouth. (Movie choices: *West Side Story* or *Viva Zapata.*)

Sample Menu 3: The Beach Party. Pack a cooler with your favorite soft drinks and wine coolers, and throw in a few Snickers bars for later. Make sandwiches (tuna, ham, PB&J) and potato salad. Don't forget the chips in assorted varieties. Stay in your bathrobe. Don't forget the sunglasses. (Movie choice: Any Elvis or Gidget movie.)

MALE TIP: If she's in the kitchen, stay out. Do not, under any circumstances, watch her eat.

The Public Pig-Out

Here are some sample menus for pigging out in public, or with a few of your closest friends experiencing the same hormonal cravings.

Sample Menu 1: Shuffle Off to Buffalo. Buffalo, New York, that is. In case you weren't aware, there's a large Italian-American population in this northeastern metropolis. Grab a friend and head for the cheesiest Italian restaurant in town, the kind that serves huge portions with nothing but heavy red sauce on everything. Eat loads of Buffalo mozzarella just for its namesake (not to mention dairy calories), fried calamari with marinara sauce, lasagna, and tiramisu. Cheap Chianti or a delicious demitasse of espresso will finish this off nicely.

Sample Menu 2: The Mediterranean. Head for the nearest Middle eastern fast-food joint or, more realistically, the deli section of the best market you can find. Purchase large quantities of the following:

Hummus
Babba ganoush

Stuffed grape leaves
Falafels
Pita bread
Greek wine
Spanikopita

Go down to the closest marina or, if you happen to be land-locked, the closest pond will do. Spread out a picnic blanket and your feast. Play Greek music and break plates as you stuff your face with some of the fattiest food in the universe. How do you think it got all that great flavor?

Sample Menu 3: The Mardi Gras. The only thing wilder than your appetite right now is Carnivale. Mardi Gras. So why not celebrate with the party experts, down home in New Orleans? Order the following from a Cajun restaurant, or if you're lucky, you may find some of the following in your grocer's deli.

Cajun popcorn (deep fried shrimp or crawfish bits)
Seafood gumbo
Crab cakes
Blackened anything, e.g., fish, steak, chicken (if you don't have Cajun spices, just overcook it until it's burned to a crisp)
Jambalaya
Cajun martinis (Martinis with jalapeno-soaked olives—yikes!)

Too much of a good thing is wonderful.

—*Mae West*

The Sweet Feast

Sometimes we want break all the rules—so why not pig out on dessert? Thus, was born: The Sweet Feast Desperado Feast. You can use any variety (as long as the portions are large) of your favorite desserts, but in case you aren't thinking clearly right now, we'll give you a sample of just the kind of feast we mean.

Mud pie (brownies covered in ice cream, hot fudge, and nuts).

Strawberries (to dip into the hot fudge after each bite of mud pie).

Sugar cookies—you need a little more crunch, and sugar cookies have a mellow enough taste to go with anything.

Hunk of New York cheesecake—for that creamy cream desire. Take a bite of this, then shove some hot fudge and a strawberry in your mouth (yes, all at once). Sheer bliss.

So forget the meat and potatoes; who cares about nutrition when you feel like this? We're certain that a dose of sugar-coated entrées will alter your mood and keep you as sweet as pie.

MALE TIP: Do not mention that she left the iron in the refrigerator.

Hurl and Rage

Sometimes when you've got PMS, you just get a wave of rage and nothing can ease your tension like hurling something across the room. *Nothing* is so satisfying. It is sort of like the times when you're really mad and only the "F" word will do. In view of this, we've come up with a list of creative "hurl-ables" for your tossing pleasure.

Food to Throw:
Tomatoes (especially rotten)
Hard biscuits
Canned foods
Things that splatter (raw eggs are a favorite)
Coffee filter with used wet grounds, crumpled in a ball
Anything you've attempted to cook which didn't work
Old gnocchi
Pie—fruit or cream (Charlie Chaplin knew what he was
     doing when he threw these)

Other Dramatic Throwables:
Any kind of glass which shatters on contact
Fine china
A photo of him
A flower vase (with flowers; water spillage)
CDs, 8-track tapes, cassettes
Lamps
That gift he just bought you
Puzzles (1000 pieces are the best)
Walnuts (in their shells)

HAPPY HURLING!

Telltale PMS Symptom: You take more baths. Water immer-sion seems important.

7

CRAMPING YOUR STYLE

~ ~ ~ ~ ~ ~

Jen's Curried Lentil Soup
Mushroom Soup
Potato Soup
Banana Pudding
Good Girls' Gaspacho
Mellow Melon Soup
Chocolate Milk Shake
Hot and Sour Soup
Carrot Ginger Soup
Black Bean Soup
Chicken Noodle Soup

~ ~ ~

Ohhhhhhhh . . . Ooooooh . . . They're heeeere. You've no longer got PMS; you've got PAIN. Cramps. Razor-sharp knives piercing into your side, fiery hot torturous jabs in your belly that send you racing for your bed . . . or the painkillers. There are women who get them so bad, they can't get out of bed for days. Some women swear labor pains are a breeze next to the horrific discomfort of cramps. And then, some women don't get them at all. If you're one of these lucky ladies, feel free to go back to the chocolate chapter. But for the Princesses of Pain, read on. Because even though you'd certainly rather wallow in self-pity with a heating pad and a bottle of Scotch, you really do need a good, healthy meal in your tender tummy. Even the most brutal pain won't keep you from sampling the warm, soothing soups and creamy, comforting puddings in this chapter. The following light, simple, and delicious dishes will not only nourish and calm you, but may even bring a smile back to your beautiful face. [NOTE: If you have a significant other or an understanding child or friend, these recipes are easy enough for anyone to prepare.] One last thing to remember about cramps . . . they can't last forever (can they?).

~ Jen's Curried Lentil Soup ~

Crawl into a bowl of this spicy-but-soothing soup. Serve with mango chutney, naan, and pakoras if they're easily available.

1 medium onion, chopped
olive oil
2 cloves garlic, chopped
1 teaspoon crumbled dried oregano
2 cups dried lentils
3 quarts chicken stock
2 carrots, chopped
pinch of fines herbes
salt
pepper
curry powder (1 tablespoon, more to taste)

Sauté onion in olive oil, add garlic (be careful not to let it burn!). Add oregano, lentils, chicken stock, chopped carrots, and fines herbes. Bring to a boil, then reduce heat and simmer for 1½ hours, until lentils are soft. Add more broth if it gets too thick. Add salt, pepper, and curry powder to taste. If you've got the energy and one of those mini–food processors, ladle some of the lentil soup into it and puree. When added to the rest of the soup, it lends a creamier texture, which is exactly what you need right now. Can be refrigerated or frozen until your next bout of cramps may even prevent you from performing the above. Rent *A Passage to India* and eat soup while it's hot. Wash down with ice cold water, or ice cold vodka, depending on your pain threshold.

ALT: One can of Progresso Lentil Soup. ½ teaspoon curry powder, ½ teaspoon cumin powder. Heat, mix, eat.

MALE TIP: Don't tease the tiger.

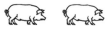

~ Mushroom Soup ~

Rich, hot, and full of flavor, this is a far cry from Campbell's. It will not only help you get through a cold, cramp-ridden day, but also makes a perfect starter for an elegant dinner. You can also puree pecans or hazelnuts into it at the last minute if you're feeling adventurous.

2 pounds fresh mushrooms (wild mixture, if possible)
½ onion, chopped
1 clove garlic, chopped
3 tablespoons unsalted butter
3 tablespoons sherry or white wine (or anything you've got handy, other than rubbing alcohol)
2 tablespoons all-purpose flour
2 quarts beef or chicken stock (Knorr's cubes or Swanson's canned broths are fine—you're in no condition to prepare Martha Stewart–perfect homemade stock)
salt
pepper
pinch of nutmeg
2 tablespoons dried thyme
2 tablespoons cream (optional)

Clean mushrooms, chop 'em up (toss the stems). Sauté onions and garlic in butter. Add mushrooms and wine and sauté some more, about five minutes. Stir in flour and stir for a minute or two longer. Add stock and bring soup to a boil. Reduce to simmer, add salt, pepper, nutmeg, and thyme. Simmer for 15–20 minutes. If you're into extra calories, add a smidgen of cream at the last minute, stir, and serve hot with some really good bread. You should feel better by now.

ALT: Put Knorr's bouillon cube (any flavor) into your mouth, add warm water. Gargle and swallow.

If only one could tell true love from false love as one can tell mushrooms from toadstools.
—*Katherine Mansfield*

~ Potato Soup ~

This creamy, flavorful soup will soothe and delight even those who've never experienced cramps.

2 pounds potatoes, diced
1 medium onion, chopped
2 stalks celery, chopped
½ stick butter
2 cups chicken broth
1–2 cups milk (to taste)
water (optional)
salt and pepper, to taste
fresh parsley

Sauté potatoes, onion, and celery in butter. Add chicken stock and milk and simmer until potatoes are completely tender. Puree some of the potatoes and add back into the soup mixture. Add water if mixture gets too thick. Season with salt and pepper, toss some chopped parsley on top. *Mmm-mmm good.*

ALT: Campbell's Potato Soup with those little oyster crackers. You'll feel like you're in the first grade again.

MALE TIP: Let her pick the video. Even if it's Showboat *and you've seen it before.*

~ Banana Pudding ~

Not too filling, just the right thing for your aching tummy. It feels so smooth going down.

1 can sweetened condensed milk (Eagle Brand)
1½ cups cold water
1 package vanilla pudding
1 carton Cool Whip
vanilla wafers (about 2 cups)
3 or more bananas

Combine condensed milk and water, add pudding, and beat well. Chill for five minutes. Fold in Cool Whip. Spoon some of the pudding mixture into a bowl and top with wafers, bananas and more pudding. This old favorite can't help but make you forget about the C-word. Eat as much as you can, but beware: If you eat too much, you'll have a different kind of stomachache.

ALT: Chop a banana up and shove it into one of those Swiss Miss vanilla pudding cups. Crumble in a few vanilla wafers for crunch.

MALE TIP: Give her a hug.

~ *Good Girls' Gaspacho* ~

Light, cool, and fresh as a cucumber, gaspacho is the perfect meal when PMS shows up in the heat of the summer to cramp your style. If you've got a blender, you can prepare the following. Just make sure that all the ingredients are fresh and you can't go wrong.

4 cups tomato juice
1 small onion, coarsely chopped
2 cups diced tomatoes
½ cup green bell pepper
½ cup red bell pepper
1 diced cucumber
1 clove garlic
dash of cumin
dash of Tabasco
2 tablespoons olive oil
2 tablespoons red wine vinegar
juice of ½ lemon and 1 lime
1 tablespoon sugar
salt and crushed black pepper, to taste

Puree all of the above in a blender (watch your fingers). Pour into a bowl and serve with garlic croutons. Weep a little bit. Get someone cute to rub your tummy.

ALT: You could have a V8.

In my sex fantasy, nobody ever loves me for my mind.
—Nora Ephron

~ Mellow Melon Soup ~

Another perfect soup when things get too hot in the kitchen. Not only will this soothe your aching belly, it also makes a great dessert for friends and family. As long as the idea of cold green soup doesn't scare you, this will soon be a favorite.

4 cups ripe honeydew melon
2 cups orange or apple juice
⅓ cup fresh lime or lemon juice
⅓ cup or more sugar
2 cups fruity white wine
big pinch of fresh mint

Throw above ingredients into a blender and set it on PULVERIZE until it's smooth or you've got your PMS angst out. Chill in refrigerator. Garnish with mint and serve it in your cutest little bowls. If it's just you, you can just dump it straight from the blender into your mouth. A refreshing, nutritious meal that is as easy to eat as it is to make.

ALT: Make a smoothie using fruit (bananas, strawberries, peaches, etc.), apple juice, and ice or frozen yogurt or ice cream. Blend.

Success for me is having ten honeydew melons and eating only the top half of each one.

—*Barbra Streisand*

~ Chocolate Milk Shake ~

Okay, so it's not really a balanced meal, but sometimes, it's the only thing you want or need when the cramps have you camped out in your bed. If you don't have a blender by now, buy one, because this creamy shake is sure to cure even the worst tummyache.

1 big glob of chocolate Häagen-Dazs (half a pint)
1 cup whole milk (forget the nonfat or even 2%—in fact, pick up a gallon of half and half)
1 huge squirt of Hershey's chocolate syrup
1 handful almonds (optional, if you like a little crunch in your shake)
1 dash vanilla
another spoonful of Häagen-Dazs for good measure

Blend all ingredients together until they have a thick, creamy consistency. If you like a thin shake, add some more milk. If you like to eat it with a spoon, by all means, dump in the rest of the ice cream. Dump the whole thing into a tall, iced mug and slurp it really loudly with a thick straw. Feel sorry for yourself and moan every once in a while, especially if someone else is in earshot. Have seconds.

ALT: Go to your local soda fountain and have them make one. Bring your boyfriend and drink it together. Make that annoying end-of-shake-straw-sucking sound. Have seconds.

If women ran the world, there wouldn't be war, just every month a few days of serious negotiations.

—*Anonymous*

~ Hot and Sour Soup ~

Hey sourpuss, get over it. This soup matches your mood. We like it extra hot. It makes us feel cooler by comparison. Now go make some soup.

8 cups water
1 ounce dried black mushrooms
3 tablespoons dry sherry
½ cup and 2 tablespoons cider vinegar
2 tablespoons soy sauce
1¾ teaspoons salt
¼ pound tofu, cut into thin strips
2 tablespoons cornstarch
2 eggs, lightly beaten
8 minced scallions
toasted sesame oil, to taste

Boil about 2 cups of the water. Pour over the mushrooms and let soak for 30 minutes. (Squish mushrooms with your fingers. The sponginess of the mushrooms will absorb your stress.)

Slice soaked mushrooms and add, with soaking liquid, to 6 cups of boiling water. Add sherry, vinegar, soy sauce, salt, and tofu. Simmer ten minutes.

In a small bowl, combine cornstarch with 1 cup of hot soup, whisking constantly until smooth. (This part is fun. Enjoy the thickening process.) Add to soup, stirring. Drizzle in eggs, stirring. Add scallions. Serve in a large bowl, adding sesame oil to taste.

ALT: Make some tea. Pretend it's soup. Order a pizza. Break up with your boyfriend because he didn't bring food home.

Anything you put in your mouth during this time is PMS food.

—F. Horstman

~ Carrot Ginger Soup ~

Soothe. Ahhh. Release. It's a great feeling! How corny can we get? Since the ginger in this soup will give you a nice calm, we thought we'd test your patience. How'd we score? On a scale from 1 to 10. Did you say scale? Get on one. That'll really aggravate you. Have some soup. Bitch.

2 pounds carrots, peeled and chopped
5 cups vegetable or chicken stock
1 teaspoon salt
2 medium onions
3 tablespoons freshly grated ginger
3–4 tablespoons butter
1 bunch cilantro (optional)

In a large stock pot, combine carrots, stock, and salt. Boil until carrots are soft, about 10–15 minutes.

In a skillet, sauté onions and ginger in butter until onions are translucent. Puree in a blender, with cilantro if desired, until everything is smooth. Return to stock pot. Heat and serve.

ALT: Eat a raw carrot and sprinkle some powdered ginger on it. Pretend you're Bugs Bunny. Say, "What's up, Doc?" The carrot chewing motion will help you get out some aggression.

In the Kasai, a part of the Congo, a woman believes that if she were to enter the forest during her monthly period, the men's hunting would fail.

> *—Man, Myth & Magic,*
> *Marshall Cavendish Corporation,*
> *New York*

~ Black Bean Soup ~

A quick way to feel warm and comfy inside. And full. A whole pot of mildly spicy Tex-Mex goodness, we're sure this will become a PMS favorite.

2 cups uncooked black beans
6 cups water
2 bay leaves
2 sunflower oil
2 medium onions chopped
4 cloves garlic
1 cup diced carrot
½ teaspoon cumin seed
1 teaspoon basil
¼ teaspoon celery seed
dash cayenne pepper
¼ cup minced fresh parsley or cilantro
Juice of 1 large lemon
Salt to taste
1–2 cups additional water as needed

Clean, wash, and soak beans in water 7–10 hours. (See that the occasional stone is removed.)

Cook beans in a covered soup pot on medium heat, simmering 1½ –2 hours. Pour half of the beans in a blender and puree. Return to heat and add bay leaves. Simmer uncovered.

In a large skillet, heat oil and sauté onions, garlic, carrot, cumin, basil, celery seed, and cayenne until vegetables are tender. Add to beans with parsley, lemon juice, and salt. Add 1–2 cups of water to thin the soup to taste. Cook another ½ hour, stirring occasionally. Serve with sour cream.

ALT: Open a can of black beans. Pour into a sauce pan. Heat. Add some spices. Add water if you want.

Telltale PMS Symptom: Your cat is the only one who understands you.

~ Chicken Noodle Soup ~

Hey "syndrome" sufferer. Feeling nauseous? Feeling sick? Fed up? Tired? Throwing tomatoes at Oprah? Calm down. We've got just the thing. Mom's chicken noodle soup. Call up a friend and have her make it. Or make her go to the deli and bring you some.

1 chicken (3½ –4 pounds), rinsed
2 onions, quartered
4 celery stalks
4 carrots
1 potato, diced
5 large mushrooms, sliced
3 parsnips
3 cloves garlic
¼ cup parsley
5 sprigs dill
salt and pepper to taste
pinch of fines herbes
3 quarts of water
1 pound of cooked fettucine (or other noodles)

Stuff a chicken into the biggest pot you've got. Toss in the rest of the ingredients. We don't care what order. Bring to a boil, reduce, and simmer for 1½–2 hours. Skim off scummy (but delicious) foam that forms.

Remove chicken and cut it up into little pieces. Strain bones out, reserving vegetables. Add chicken, reserved veggies, and cooked noodles. Heat for 2 minutes. Serve immediately.

ALT: We went for the nostalgic standby: Campbell's Chicken Noodle Soup. Buy a case or so, line the cans up, and create your own living Warhol.

No mean woman can cook well, for it calls for a light head, a generous spirit and a large heart.

—Paul Gauguin

8

COMPLEXION DISTRESS FOODS

~ ~ ~ ~ ~ ~

Avocado/Banana Mask
Oatmeal/Apple Mask
Mayonnaise Mask
Yogurt Mask
Cucumber/Honey/Milk Mask
Fruit Gel Masks
Our Favorite Store-Bought Masks

~ ~ ~

Hey, pizza face. We've all been there.

It's the night before the big benefit, you can hardly fit into the gown you bought two weeks ago, your manicure is already ruined, and now you've got a big zonker in the middle of your forehead. Sexy.

Pimples, zits, blackheads . . . we don't want to gross you out, but during these premenstrual days, like your body, your face is taking a good beating.

Some simple suggestions: Stop picking. Hide the mirrors. Get out the cover stick and apply liberally.

We've included some holistic facial remedies which you may find useful (and distracting) during this psychologically trying time.

Apply these masks liberally, and if you feel like it, apply to the rest of your body. You've done something good for yourself. Now go eat the rest of the chocolate chip cookies.

Nobody can make you feel inferior without your consent.
—Eleanor Roosevelt

Facials

If you can't get to your favorite salon for the deluxe European facial, we've decided to give you some homemade alternatives. First, bring a big pot of water to a boil. Turn off heat, and holding a towel over your head, steam your face for ten minutes. Clean out pores and apply one of the following masks. Sit back, put cucumber slices on your eyelids, and dream. Follow with ice-cold water and your favorite moisturizer. Don't you feel better already?

~ Avocado/Banana Mask ~ (for dry skin)

1 avocado, mushed   **1 banana, mushed**

Slather on your face and leave on for 20–30 minutes. Scare your boyfriend. Finally your exterior will resemble your interior.

~ Oatmeal/Apple Mask ~ (for oily skin)

⅔ cup cooked oatmeal   **¼ cup applesauce or**
1 egg white   **finely grated apples**

Apply to face and leave on until oatmeal is good and crusty.

~ Mayonnaise Mask ~

½ cup mayonnaise

Leave on face for 15 minutes. Feel the new creamy complexion.

~ Yogurt Mask ~

½ cup yogurt

Leave on for 15 minutes.

~ Cucumber/Honey/Milk Mask ~

2 tablespoons honey
¼ cup milk
½ cucumber, grated

Mix ingredients, apply to face. This will make a mess. How good it is.

MALE TIP: Do not react to the weird-looking junk on her face. Kiss her anyway.

~ Fruit Gel Masks ~

1 envelope Knox gelatin
½ cup fruit juice

In a nonreactive pan or oven-proof glass bowl, heat gelatin and juice until gelatin is dissolved. Cool in fridge for 30 minutes. Apply to face.

For oily skin, use grapefruit or lemon juice. For normal to dry skin, try apple, pear, or raspberry juice.

~ Our Favorite Store-Bought Masks

Decleor Clay and Herbal Mask
Borghese Spa Mud Mask (the green stuff)
Dermologica Clay Mask
Reviva Mask au Placenta (for extremely dry skin)

My true friends have always given me that supreme proof of devotion. A spontaneous aversion for the man I loved.
—Colette

9
RECOVERY

~ ~ ~ ~ ~ ~ ~

Fruit Salad with Fat-Free Raspberry Sauce
Angel Hair with Tomatoes and Basil
Hard-Core Steamed Veggies and Rice
Tabouli
Spinach and Mushroom Salad
Blueberry Bran Muffins
Salmon en Papillote
Jen and Fritzi's Grilled Chicken
Baked Potato
Madi's Beet and Potato
Julia's Low-Cal/High-Taste Vinaigrette

~ ~ ~

Finally, the sun glistens from behind the dark cloud of PMS. It's over; and you're a normal, healthy, and astonishingly happy woman again. You were certain that the gloom and depression were here to stay, that your life really was a complete and total disaster. And that your friends and family (especially your spouse) were all plotting against you. But your mind is suddenly clear and you realize . . . maybe it *was* just the hormones. God forbid anyone suggest such a thing while you were in the midst of PMS, but deep down inside, you can admit it to yourself. Maybe you were just a *teeny* bit irrational when you threw that tantrum over your missing hairbrush. Ahh, but now it's over and another bout of life's most mysterious mood wrecker has passed through and you are victorious (that is, if you haven't been hospitalized). If you've followed our recipes, you've taken ample advantage of your condition and indulged your cravings with wild abandon, so you probably need a few recovery tips. We have a hunch that you know enough about grapefruit and dry toast to last you a lifetime, so we've come up with a few of our favorites, some "on the road to recovery" meals such as spinach and mushroom salad, and some hard-core recovery dishes such as fruit salad with fat-free raspberry sauce. In fact, the following recipes are so delicious that you may just head straight for this chapter the next time PMS comes knocking at your door. Healthy eating!

A period is just the beginning of a lifelong sentence.
—Cathy Crimmins

~ Fruit Salad with Fat-Free Raspberry Sauce ~

Fruit salads always make us feel healthy and as if we're at a spa. Try one of our facial masks (*see* chapter 8, "Complexion Distress Foods") while casually eating your fruit salad. You're such a good girl!

banana
mixed berries (raspberries, blueberries,
   strawberries, who cares)
Bosc pear
peach
honeydew melon
raspberries (fresh or frozen, thawed)
sugar

Fruit

Slice and cube all fruit except raspberries, however you would most like to devour it. If you can't find some of the above, substitutions are absolutely allowed, in fact, encouraged. You've really come through this time; you deserve it.

Sauce

Put raspberries in a blender, with sugar to taste. Start with a tablespoon and go from there. There is no fat in sugar, so go to town, unless you've got a thing about cavities. Add a little water and blend. Spoon over your fruit salad and enjoy with a tall glass of spring water. You should feel as fresh as the girl on the Evian label.

ALT: You shouldn't be incapacitated at this point, but if you're just plain lazy, they've still got those little cans of fruit cocktail.

A woman is like a tea bag. You never know how strong she is until she gets into hot water.

—Eleanor Roosevelt

~ Angel Hair with Tomatoes and Basil ~

This light, elegant pasta has all the taste and none of the fat. Serve with a Chianti and a hearty French bread (without the butter).

4 Roma or other tomatoes
3 cloves garlic
fresh basil (2 tablespoon chopped, or more to taste)
1 teaspoon olive oil
Dash of red wine (optional)
Salt and pepper to taste
angel hair (cappelini) pasta

Chop tomatoes, garlic, and basil. Sauté garlic in olive oil, add tomatoes (peel them first if you've got that much energy—or just dump them in boiling water; the skins will come right off!) and basil and sauté some more. Add dash of wine, and salt and pepper. Cook your angel hair pasta until al dente (about 2 minutes). Pour sauce over pasta and eat. Even with a glass of Chianti, this is a very healthy, low-calorie meal. You should be able to fit into your jeans by now.

ALT: Don't even *think* about SpaghettiOs. Have you no shame? If you must, dump a can of Italian stewed tomatoes into a bowl, microwave, and pour over cooked pasta.

A good meal in troubled times is always that much salvaged from disaster.

—*A. J. Liebling*

~ Hard-Core Steamed Veggies and Rice ~

For those of you who have put on more than a few pounds, you may have to resort to the hard-core dishes such as this one to shed them. You probably know how to steam veggies, but seeing it in a cookbook may actually encourage you to do it. And yes, steamed veggies and rice do constitute a meal.

zucchini (any squash will do fine)
broccoli
new potatoes
mushrooms
any one or more of your personal favorite veggies
rice

Chop veggies up and put them in a steamer with water on the bottom *(duh)*. Steam until tender. Follow the directions on rice. We like wild rice, but white or brown rice will do. (Note: Do *not* use Rice-A-Roni. This will only throw you back into Fatsville again!). Spoon steamed veggies over rice. You can use a little soy sauce, but watch out for the sodium unless you want to bloat up all over again.

ALT: If you've got the presence of mind to go for such a healthy meal, you can handle the above recipe.

MALE TIP: Don't ask questions.

~ Tabouli ~

A light, refreshing salad that is low in calories and high in parsley.

1 cup dry bulgur wheat
1½ cups boiling water
1 teaspoon salt
¼ cup fresh lemon juice
2 teaspoons minced garlic
¼ cup olive oil
⅓ cup chopped scallions
2 tomatoes, chopped
¾ cups parsley, packed and chopped
¾ cups fresh mint, chopped

Throw bulgur wheat, boiling water, and salt in a bowl. Cover and let stand at least 20 minutes, until water is absorbed. Add lemon juice, garlic, oil, and mix thoroughly. Chill for 1 hour.

Add scallions, tomatoes, parsley, and mint to wheat. Let flavors blend for another hour before serving.

You've got to have something to eat and a little love in your life before you can hold still for any damn body's sermon on how to behave.

—*Billie Holiday*

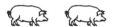

~ Spinach and Mushroom Salad ~

This dish is so healthy and full of iron, it'll make you as strong as Popeye. It's low in fat, so if you eat enough of these, you may just get as thin as Olive Oyl.

1 pound baby spinach leaves (you can use the prewashed and bagged variety)
10–15 mushrooms
2 tablespoons minced red onion (or Maui, if in season)
your choice vinaigrette dressing (vinegar and olive oil)
1 boiled egg, cut in wedges

Clean spinach well by letting it soak in a sink full of water until all the dirt is gone (once again, you might want to use prewashed and bagged spinach). Dry spinach. Clean and slice mushrooms. Sauté onion and vinaigrette for 1 minute. Remove pan from heat and add spinach and egg wedges. Toss to coat with dressing and mushrooms. (If you're not into recovery, you can use the old version, which calls for crumbled bacon, but it's just as delicious without it.)

A woman may develop wrinkles and cellulite, lose her waistline, her bustline, her ability to bear a child, even her sense of humor, but none of that implies a loss of her sexuality, her femininity . . .

—*Barbara Gordon*

~ Blueberry Bran Muffins ~

Moist, delicious, and about the healthiest breakfast you could ever wish for, these muffins will soon become a regular craving even in the midst of your PMS.

2 cups bran flakes
½ cup boiling water
1 cup buttermilk
1 cup blueberries
¼ cup brown sugar
½ stick butter
3½ tablespoons molasses
2 tablespoons banana, mashed
2 eggs
1 cup whole wheat flour
¾ teaspoon baking soda
¼ teaspoon salt

Preheat oven to 350°.

Butter muffin pan and dust with flour. Mix bran and boiling water together. Add buttermilk and blueberries. Cream brown sugar, butter, molasses, mashed banana, eggs, and flour together. Beat together well (you can use an electric mixer for this part), then add to bran mixture and blend lightly. Pour mixture into muffin pan and bake 20–30 minutes. Do not overcook—they should be slightly soft. Absolutely fabulous!

MALE TIP: This is not the time to mention that her old hairdo made her face look thinner.

~ Salmon en Papillote ~

Steaming fish and veggies inside cute little pouches of foil or parchment paper are not only healthy and delicious, but fun! Feel free to vary the fish and the veggies, but remember that some vegetables need to be slightly precooked, as the cooking time is so short. Invite some of your other PMS-recovering pals over for this meal—they, of all people, will appreciate its beauty and simplicity.

1 salmon filet
1 thinly sliced leek
1 thinly sliced red or yellow bell pepper
½ thinly sliced potato (slightly precooked)
1 tablespoon fresh dill
**1 tablespoon white wine (or dab of olive oil or
    butter)**

Cut a piece of foil or parchment paper into a rectangle or heart shape. Arrange filet in center, along with veggies. Add wine and fold remaining half of foil or parchment over the fish and seal the package by folding the edges. Cook the package at 400° for 8–12 minutes (depending on size of filet).

Men are taught to apologize for their weaknesses, women for their strengths.

—*Lois Wyse*

~ Jen and Fritzi's Grilled Chicken ~

This dish will fill you up and please your palate. Remember to properly food combine. No rice or potatoes with this chicken. Vegetables only.

3 tablespoons olive oil
2 tablespoons balsamic vinegar
2 tablespoons lemon juice
1 clove garlic, crushed
1 tablespoon dried rosemary
dash of honey, to taste
salt and pepper to taste
2 skinned chicken breasts (one for tomorrow)

Mix marinade. Coat both sides of chicken breasts with marinade. Put in fridge for 2 hours, or overnight if you can wait that long.

Place chicken on a hot grill or in your broiler. Cook 3 minutes on each side. Check center to make sure the pink is gone.

Serve with steamed vegetables or tomato slices.

No [wo] man can be wise on an empty stomach.

—*George Eliot*

~ Baked Potato ~

Yeah. Like you don't know how to bake a potato. It's a dish which is almost filling by itself, and with the delightful toppings below, you might even forget you're in "recovery."

1 Idaho potato

Preheat oven to 375°
Scrub potato. Prick several times with a fork. Bake directly on the rack for 1—1½ hours. Serve immediately.

Suggested Toppings:

cottage cheese
butter and sour cream (you know what you're doing)
broccoli and cheese
sautéed mushrooms and onions
caramelized onions
yogurt
salsa
avocado
black beans and salsa

The way I see it, if you want the rainbow you gotta put up with the rain.

—*Dolly Parton*

～ Madi's Beet and Potato ～

A strange, but delicious dish. Beets are rich in vitamins. Don't use a lot of sour cream or you'll be back to square one. Fritzi's sister, an expert PMS sufferer, makes this when she feels better.

Boil a beet and a potato (about 30 minutes). Peel them. Chop them up in a bowl. Add salt, pepper, and sour cream. Eat.

Yum.

ALT: You just read it.

The trouble with being in the rat race is that even if you win, you're still a rat.

—*Lily Tomlin*

~ Julia's Low-Cal/High-Taste Vinaigrette ~

For years, no one knew the secret to our friend Julia's amazing salad dressing. The secret is in the maple syrup, which takes the tartness out of the vinegar. Sorry, Jules, now the world knows.

½ cup olive oil
¼ cup balsamic vinegar
2 cloves crushed garlic
1 teaspoon maple syrup
dash of salt and pepper to taste
prewashed mixed greens

Mix all dressing ingredients in a cruet or jar with a lid. Shake. Toss with prewashed mixed greens and other wonderful veggies, if you wish.

What's the difference between worry and panic? About 28 days.

—*Anonymous*

MORE TELLTALE SYMPTOMS OF PMS

You cry in traffic.

You cry when you change the cat litter.

You cry when your boyfriend brings you flowers.

You cry because you don't have a boyfriend to bring you flowers.

You cry because the postman has to walk in the snow.

You cry because the checkout girl was so sweet.

You plot the demise of the other checkout girl, the evil one.

You worry about being abducted by aliens.

You go into a hysterical rage when you misplace your keys.

You cry when you hear an ambulance go by.

You cry for all the orphans in the world.

You cry at the sight of any baby.

You yell at telephone solicitors. Then cry.

You wear socks to bed.

Those weird little growls you make scare your dog.

You cry when you take out the garbage.

You cry when you spill the garbage.

You cry because you can't figure out the recycling thing.

You just went grocery shopping and there's nothing to eat.

You just went grocery shopping and you didn't buy anything.

You just went grocery shopping and you cry.

You can't tell if you're voiding your bowels or your
bladder.

You've found a common bond with the Michelin Tire Man.

Nothing fits.

You cry to any song on the radio.

Your dog doesn't recognize you.

Plates and utensils are optional.

You run out of cover-up. You cry.

Life seems more confusing than usual.

Life seems even more pointless than ever.

You're suddenly crying again.

You've just run out of Kleenex.

You cry.